Wicca For Beginners

BOOK OF WICCA SPELLS AND WITCHCRAFT FOR BEGINNERS

By Samantha Lisa

Table of Contents

Introduction 1

Chapter 1: An Introduction to Wicca 3

Chapter 2: Wiccan Beliefs 18

Chapter 3: The God and the Goddess 32

Chapter 4: The Wheel of the Year 47

Chapter 5: The Magic of Wicca........................... 90

Chapter 6: A Beginner's Grimoire – Basic Spells

to Master 141

Chapter 7: A Glossary of Magical

Correspondences 170

Conclusion... 191

Introduction

Congratulations on downloading *Wicca For Beginners* and thank you for doing so.

The following chapters will discuss the origins and history of the modern religion of Wicca, as well as where it's most popular and where it is practiced. *Wicca For Beginners* will discuss the founding thinkers who pieced together from ancient, arcane knowledge the building blocks of neo-paganism and Wicca, as well as the belief system and 13 defining attributes that make a Wiccan unique.

This book will cover the sabbaths and lunar esbats of the Wheel of the Year, and why they are so important to Wiccans, as well as the magical altar tools of Wicca, what they symbolize, and how they are used. *Wicca For Beginners* will introduce the aspiring witch to the concepts of magic, raising energy, casting a circle, and performing rituals and magic. The power of the five Elements will be covered, and the magical properties of herbs, crystals, candle colors and days of the week will be explained.

Spells for the beginning witch are provided to help in all areas of life, including money and wealth, good luck and prosperity, love and beauty, and protection and healing.

Finally, a glossary of magical correspondences finishes the book with a handy go-to reference guide to herbs, plants, and crystals.

There are plenty of books on this subject on the market, thanks again for choosing this one! Every effort was made to ensure it is full of as much useful information as possible, please enjoy!

Chapter 1: An Introduction to Wicca

Wicca's History

In the late 19th century, scholars of ancient folklore, authors of history, and a British civil servant produced several books and offered ideas as to how some of the known, ancient pagan practices of Ireland, Wales, and Scotland could be revisited and rejuvenated into a modern religion.

Besides the works of these three individuals, Wicca itself might have never returned to the world's consciousness. There is hard and fast proof that pagan practices of the ancient Celts and Druids existed—all we have are archaeological ruins, artifacts, and the numerous legends, myths, and practices that have survived, secretly woven into modern British, Scottish and Irish society, and that have been carried over to the Americas. Carving Jack-o-lanterns originated as a practice of farmers carving out the middles of turnips and placing stumps of candles in them, to light the way of any lost spirits on All Hallow's Eve. Weaving Brigid's crosses from grass, making corn dollies, jumping bonfires, leaving a plate for the dead at a mute supper, and countless centuries of herbal knowledge prove to us that *something* existed before modern industrial times. Most of us have heard a superstition or odd bit of folklore from a grandparent, such as always close a pair of scissors, or putting a pair of shoes on the table will invite the *banshee*. There is a curiosity in modern times, a yearning for arcane knowledge and to understand the mysteries of the natural world. Wicca provides a fertile landscape on which to plant our private hopes and dreams, and allows us the freedom to be ourselves, delightfully human, and in the form and guidance of the God and Goddess, always forgiving, always guiding.

With such a heady potential for freedom, magical knowledge, and a strong sense of community, it's no wonder that Wicca rises in popularity each year.

Wicca's Founding Leaders

Gerald Gardner, a British native, first joined a witch's coven in 1939, and this would inspire him to write about what he perceived to be the Old Religion. Drawing upon wisdom from Eastern faiths, as well as teachings and practices of the Freemasons, he went on to author books called " Witchcraft Today" and " The Meaning of

Witchcraft". These books have been essential in providing a blueprint for what Wicca is today throughout the world. Additionally, the Gardnerian path is one of the formal means of education for Wiccans to follow, making the claim that it links modern students to ancient Druidic and Celtic matriarchal faiths and practices.

Charles Leland is another of the founding persons of modern-day Wicca. He is best known for his book " Aradia – Gospel of the Witches", which he stated was inspired by Diana, a moon goddess. Finally, the author Margaret Murray published books that brought the persecution of witches by the Catholic and Protestant churches to light, providing insight as to why there are no existing formal pagan cultures left from ancient times, nor is there a written tradition. To live openly as a witch, until now, has always proven quite dangerous.

These pioneers are no longer with us, but their legacies are what put Wicca on the map. Today there are approximately 15 million practicing Wiccans throughout the world; Wicca is one of the fastest-growing religions after Buddhism and Islam.

A New, Old Religion

Because the ancient pagans of Europe possessed an oral, not written, history, it has always been difficult to prove that Wicca or any other neo-pagan faith is based on actual ancient culture. However, archaeological discoveries have helped modern scholars understand that at some point in Europe's history, worshippers followed a male hunter deity and a mother goddess, as well as a Sun god. Images depicting a horned man, sporting antlers of a stag from his shaggy head, point to this, as well as images of a pregnant, female figure.

Wicca is referred to as the Old Religion, the Craft of the Wise, or simply, " The Craft". Its practitioners strive to march forward, away from the persecution and terror of the past, and onward to a joyful and jubilant embracing of a safer, proud future. It takes a lot of work to detach the maligned image of a witch from the slander the medieval Catholic church committed during the 15th through the 18th centuries. Even Hollywood has done little to remove the stigma from the natural folk-healer and magical practitioner. This was part of the thought process regarding the name " Wicca"; Wicca is merely the following of the natural change of seasons, the moon, and life surrounding harvest, as well as the practice of witchcraft, however, " witchcraft" as a name of a faith was thought to be too potentially inflammatory, so Wiccan was chosen as the faith's name.

Witchcraft throughout Europe was initially persecuted because of the rise of modern medicine; when the men involved in promoting new ideas in medicine came to power, matriarchal herbalists paid the price. Now in the face of the many faults (as well as expenses) of modern Western medicine, herbalism is coming back into popularity, and with good reason.

Where Wicca Is Practiced Throughout the World

Wicca is most widely practiced in Europe, particularly the United Kingdom (which encompasses Britain, Scotland, Wales and Northern Ireland) and Southern Ireland. It is also very popular in the United States as well as Canada, however, even though it's a minority religion, it can be practiced anywhere its faithful decide to go. The United States officially recognizes Wicca as a religion, after the US Military was petitioned to allow fallen Wiccan soldiers to have pentagrams engraved on their headstones. Legally ordained Wiccan clergy exist in every US state and throughout Canada; Wiccan priests are often permitted to attend to Wiccan inmates in penitentiaries.

Dispelling Common Myths About Wicca and Modern Paganism

Of course, despite the great advances that Wicca has made in becoming a legitimate, accepted modern religion, there are still many misunderstandings and prejudices regarding this peaceful, nature-worshipping faith.

Wiccans do not believe in or acknowledge a " devil", or Satan character. The Wiccan Horned God is symbolic of the virility of nature and of the masculine, it has nothing to do with any Christian notion of evil or of the devil. They believe in the ebb and flow of the natural world, and that sometimes there is growth, and sometimes decay, but darkness is not evil—it is simply the absence of light. As they worship the departure and return of the Sun God, so do they commit themselves to the faith that even in the darkest hour, so will Light return to the world.

Wiccans disregard moral absolutes. They strive to practice their magic and their faith with a portion of humility, never seeking power over another or practicing magic that aims to directly harm or disable someone else.

Wiccans and other pagans do not seek to recruit others, for Wiccan is not a cult. It is a calling to those who wish to pursue its path, and Wiccans take personal choice very seriously.

Wiccans do not sacrifice animals. That would directly contradict their law to " Harm None".

Wiccans do not take the energy from another person in order to make their magic powerful. Wiccans and other pagans believe that we are all imbued with divine energy, as well as the potential to utilize that energy in order to practice magic and witchcraft.

Witches aren't real. Of course they are; a witch is simply a person who practices magic. (Some Wiccans and witches prefer to spell magic with a " k", i.e. *magick*, in order to differentiate it from performative stage magic. Either spelling is acceptable). A witch is a self-aware scholar of ways both ancient and modern to utilize the power of the natural world and of themselves to make changes in their lives and in themselves.

You are not a " real" witch or Wiccan without years of commitment and training. This is a personal choice; you're a witch if you practice magic, and you're a Wiccan if you decide that you are, it's as simple as that. Some Wiccans prefer to pursue their path alone, and we call these individuals " solitary" witches. Others feel more comfortable surrounded by a formal community, and to be taught by ordained elders, priests, and priestesses. There is no wrong way to be a Wiccan, so long as you adhere to the Wiccan Rede and try to practice Wiccan tenets throughout your daily life.

You need the proper tools in order to practice witchcraft. Tools are wonderful, they're fun to use and enjoyable to buy, but at the end of the day, it's a Wiccan's *mind* that enables he or she to practice magic. You can easily cast a spell with nothing more than your imagination and a stick you found in the woods.

A male witch is called a warlock. Not all witches or Wiccans are female. A male witch is simply a witch.

If your family are not witches, then neither are you. There is no pedigree needed to be a witch or a Wiccan. Wiccans and other pagans highly prize the force of one's *will*: if you desire it to be so (for yourself), then it is. It's as simple as that.

Hexes do not work. Unfortunately, any magical intention set forth into the universe will have some effect. For Wiccans, casting magic with the intention of causing someone else harm goes against everything Wicca stands for. Additionally, Wiccans strive to work their magic in tandem with nature, not against it. Causing harm for no other reason than the ego demands it is unnatural and disrespectful to the universe.

" White magic" is completely ineffective, while " black magic" is evil. This is another misconception perpetuated by Hollywood. Magic is most effective when the spellcaster is specific in their intention and works with the natural laws of the time and place the spell is cast. Magic can be used for any purpose—a healing spell cast during the new moon can bring relief to someone who's needed to get more sleep or change their diet for better digestion, and a protection spell cast during the dark moon on a Saturday can suddenly distract the originator of hurtful gossip and redirect their attention elsewhere. Nothing here is either " black" or " white", it simply works with nature and the witch's intent to produce results.

Joining a coven is a necessary part of becoming a Wiccan or a witch. It's not; a coven is a small group of individuals who come together to celebrate the sabbaths, esbats, or perform magic together. A community is larger, and less formal. And then there are individuals who prefer to practice alone—these are referred to as " solitaries".

Wiccans have orgies. Again, more Hollywood, but one thing to note is that Wiccans do believe that sex and sexuality are sacred and blessed by the divine. Some solitary practitioners or covens may prefer to be " skyclad" (without clothing) during circle, but it is not for any sexual purpose, merely to feel closer to the God and Goddess in a natural form. There are never any sexual, public rites performed at a sabbath or esbat.

The pentacle is the sign of the devil. This could not be farther from the truth. The pentagram is a symbol of a five-pointed star; it can be right-side up or upside-down, and neither represent Satan, a figure created by the Christian Church. With the single point up top, the pentagram is a symbol of the elements: Earth, Air, Fire, Water, and Spirit. It is also a symbol of humankind (if you imagine the single point is the person's head, and the other four are their arms and legs). With two points up, the pentagram is a symbol of wild nature (think a goat, stag, or ram).

How do Wiccans and Pagans differ? A Wiccan is a type of Pagan, just as a Baptist is a type of Christian. There are many different pagan faiths in the world, such as Stregha, Heathens, Feri, and Druids. The word " pagan" comes from the latin *paganus*, or " of the countryside".

Chapter 2: Wiccan Beliefs

Wiccan Values

Wicca is a religion that affords its members a significant amount of personal freedom, including what they believe. That being said, there are common beliefs and ethics that weave themselves throughout the Wiccan community.

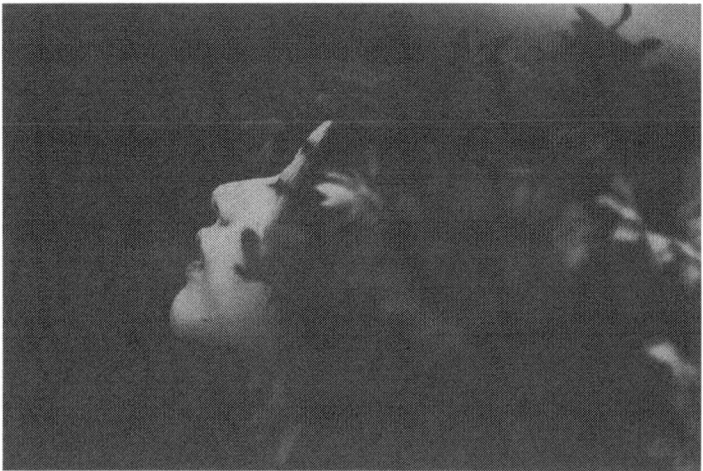

The Goddess

The Goddess is central to the Wiccan religion. While both the God and the Goddess are worshipped, the Goddess is recognized as the creator of all—She gives birth to the Earth itself as well as the gods. The idea that motherhood and matriarchy are central to life and therefore focused on in every ritual and observance is believed to have been carried forward from ancient times until present.

There is a tangible joy, a sense of relief for many Wiccans when they come into the fold and realize that the love of the Goddess is 100% unconditional. Many Wiccans were raised in Christian households, and perhaps didn't have the loving support they were after within their family's faith. In Wicca as well as in other pagan religions, the Goddess means safety, support, neverending healing and love. She will never abandon her children, and we are all her children, even the God.

Because the Goddess exists in all things, life must be understood as sacred and precious. This is why the Wiccan Rede is so important.

The Wiccan Rede

The Wiccan Rede is the most important tenet of the Wiccan religion. It states that " Do what you will, that it harm none". There are a few different variations on this, but they all mean the same thing: you have the free will to make your own choices, but please try to make choices that will not directly, negatively effect another person. Make sure your intention is benevolent, even in matters of banishment and protection.

This is why the Words of Casting are used to close every spell. These state that " By the power of three times three, I cast this spell and set it free— to do no harm, nor to bring any harm to me, I cast this spell, so mote it be."

The Rule of Three

Also called the Threefold Law, the Rule of Three states that whatever you send into the world will eventually return to you, triple the amount. It serves to remind us that for every action there is a reaction, and that we should never be careless with our power, intentions, or magic. The world certainly needs as much benevolence as it can get, so if we have to choose between reactions of love and patience and reactions of malice or rage, we should strive to choose the former, and abstain from the latter with as much strength as we possess.

What Makes a Wiccan Unique

There are 13 defining attributes of Wiccans:

1) Wiccans practice rituals in order to live according to the rhythm of nature. These are observed as the Lunar phases, the equinoxes, the solstices, and the other sabbaths.

2) Wiccans realize that human intelligence comes with a responsibility towards one's environment, therefore, Wiccans try to live in harmony with nature, with practices that benefit the environment and the evolution of all life.

3) Wiccans acknowledge the fact that through the practice of magic, they possess a power that is greater than most average persons. Although it may be called a " supernatural" ability by some, Wiccans propose that is is actually part of the

natural world, merely overlooked by non-practitioners.

4) Wiccans recognize the duality of the Universe as possessing both masculine and feminine, similar to the concepts of Yin and Yang. Neither is greater than the other; they are supportive and necessary to one another, and also exist in all humans. Wiccans look at sex and sexuality as a gift from the Goddess, and not as something to be ashamed of, so long as mutual consent is given. Sex is also a divine act and a symbol of life itself.

5) Wiccans recognize different planes of existence, such as the material world and the spirit world.

6) Wiccans do not allow an absolute hierarchy within their ranks, but they honor the teachers, elders, priests and priestesses who give their time and devote their lives to teaching future generations the Old Ways.

7) Wiccans view their practice as combining magic, religion, and nature-based wisdom. Together these elements form the Wiccan way of life.

8) A witch is such because he or she practices witchcraft, not because of lineage or false claims. Degrees and initiations are the individual's choice, but they do not determine who is a witch and who is not. A witch strives to control forces within his or herself in order to live a better life, and in greater harmony with the natural world.

9) Wiccans believe in seeking fulfillment and affirmation in their lives by seeking to give greater meaning to the Universe and by examining their individual roles within that Universe.

10) Wiccans keep no animosity towards Christianity, save for the fact that Christianity insists it is the only " true" religion, and all others are false. Wiccans have no issue with other faiths, so long as

those faiths do not strive to suppress the religious freedom of others.

11) Wiccans resist feeling threatened by other members of the Craft engaging in debate about the tenets or practices of Wicca. They welcome dialogue that seeks to further the cause of Wiccan and pave the way for the future.

12) Wiccans refute the idea of " absolute evil" and do not worship entities like " Satan" or " the Devil" as defined by Christian principles. Wiccans abhor the search for power via the suffering of others.

13) Wiccans believe that everything we need in life can be found in Nature and its mysteries.

An interesting fact: the 13 Wiccan principles are incorporated into American Army chaplains' handbooks. The American Federation of Witches, led by Carl Llewellyn Weschke, were responsible for first creating these 13 Wiccan principles; while they eventually disbanded, the work they did for the modern Wiccan community was important and enduring.

Wiccan Paths

An important aspect of the Wiccan faith to understand is the fact that there is no set way to advance in one's magical education. There are opportunities to join a formal training circle as well as the option to remain practicing as a solitary witch, or any combination of the two. Many covens offer a formal education as an option to all new members. The training is presided over by a priest or priestess, and moves slowly compared to most modern schools are trades houses. The rule of thumb is to allow the aspirant to advance to the next level of knowledge after a " year and a day", which of course is dependent on how well the witch is mastering the concepts taught to them. There is no pressure or rigid timeline, because magic is not something to be taken lightly. Unlike formal education in the mundane world, it's more important to fully absorb the knowledge than it is to advance to the next level.

The goal of a formal Wiccan training is to one day achieve the coveted spot of high priest or priestess. Rather than having power over the community, these titles instead have the honor over presiding naming ceremonies, handfastings, and cronings and sagings, as well as sabbaths and esbats. Priests and priestesses are considered helpers of the God and the Goddess, and give their service to the community in sacrifice for the benefit of all, rather than being esteemed or " higher" than any one community member. A priest or priestess must never abuse their power to influence someone else, but they are often turned to for advice, and will never turn any witch away who is seeking answers to questions.

One of the reasons it's useful for a solitary witch to occasionally celebrate a sabbath or esbat with a larger, public community or coven is the opportunity to network and talk with other witches. There's a lot to learn, and endless amounts of different insights to consider. Many large, established covens open their doors to solitary witches as long as they know another member of the coven. There is never a push to recruit a witch; joining a coven is strictly voluntary.

Wiccaning Ceremony

One of the ceremonies of Wicca is something called a " Wiccaning". It is typically when a couple first has a new baby in their life, but it can occur at any age. A wiccaning serves to introduce a person by name to the members of a Wiccan community. It is neither an endorsement of the Craft nor a promise that the person being named will join the Old Ways. It can be an introduction to the child or older person's actual name, or a Wiccan name that the child or older person has picked for themselves. Wiccans believe that children are not mature enough to choose their faith, even though they may be curious about their parents' religion, and may choose to join in community celebrations happily.

Dedication

When a person does decide to enter the Craft, however, there is usually a ceremony called simply a " dedication". The person may choose a " craft name", something unique to them and known only to other members of the coven or community. Dedications are often performed at the Imbolc sabbath, when life is new and hope is in the air for the coming Spring.

Handfasting

When a Wiccan couple chooses to join together, they may opt to partake in a ceremony called " handfasting". This is not a formal marriage, although the couple may also choose to visit a judge or clerk of court to make the union official in the eyes of the law. At a handfasting, a priest or priestess oversees the ceremony, and loosely binds cords over the couples' clasped hands and says that they will remain together " so long as their love shall last".

Handparting

Handparting is a respectful ceremony performed if a couple decides they are no longer to be together. The cords are ritually cut with an athame or boline, and some couples choose to keep the pieces as a reminder of their time together. In Wicca, there is no stigma about a relationship ending. It is merely considered the natural course of each other's particular paths.

Croning and Saging

Croning, for women, and Saging, for men, is a way to honor the elder members of the Wiccan community. Elders are beloved in Wicca, for they are the ones who've gone on before the rest of the community to learn, teach, and light the way for future generations.

Sometimes younger members of the community undergo a croning or saging ceremony, usually when they are enduring a serious injury or illness such as cancer. Such battles mature a person well before their time, and saging and croning is a way to both pay respect to the person, and preparing them for the inevitability and peace of death, if it comes earlier than expected.

Chapter 3: The God and the Goddess

Mother, Maiden, and Crone

The Triple Goddess, as She is referred to, can be observed for millenia and throughout human history, across cultures and geographical areas. A man by the name of Robert Cochrane can be given the credit for bringing the Triple Goddess into the lexicon of modern Wiccan and neo-paganism, while even legendary men such as Aleister Crowley and Sigmund Freud recognized Her in their writings. By the 1970's, the Triple Goddess had become a central figure in Wiccan worship and prayer.

The Triple Goddess is not thought of a single deity, but rather the three stages of the feminine Goddess: there is the Maiden, the Mother, and the

Crone. Each stage represents a unique aspect of life and the perspective it provides.

The Maiden

The Maiden is aligned with the New Moon to the Waxing phase of the moon. She represents innocence as well as ingenuity, daring as well as demureness. She is the Goddess before She assumes the role of matriarch, and is free to spend her days as she chooses, unburdened by family or mate.

There is a warrior-like spirit to the Maiden, and we can see that in hunter-goddesses such as Artemis. There is also the spark of the creator, and goddess who rule creativity and divine inspiration, such as Brigid, are represented by the Maiden.

The Maiden is pure potential. She is just beginning, and so blesses all apprentices, students, new love, new endeavors. She is the writer before a blank page; the painter before a new canvas, and the farmer surveying an un-tilled field at the earliest sign of Spring.

Some of the many goddesses who embody the aspect of the Maiden are: Artemis (also known as Diana), Aphrodite, Amaterasu, Brigid, Freya, Kuan Yin, Persephone, and Oshun.

The Mother

It is perhaps easiest to draw near this aspect of the Goddess and relate to Her in the role as Mother, for in doing so, we allow ourselves to be vulnerable as well as cared for. In this aspect, the Triple Goddess is at Her peak—she is akin to the full Moon, the harvest at its height, the middle of summer when life is bountiful and beautiful.

The Mother goddess is here to remind us to enjoy life. She heals our wounds and strengthen our spirits to send us back out into the world and resume our proper path. She is unconditional love, and is always there for us to whisper about our fears and our pain. She is mighty in strength yet calm in nature. She is known as the cauldron of life, and the dark red of life's blood is her hue.

The Mother goddess is aligned with the power of the full Moon.

Some of the many goddesses who embody the aspect of the Mother are: Corn Mother, Demeter, Durga, Hera, Hestia, Isis, Frigg, Yemaya, and White Buffalo Calf Woman.

The Crone

The Crone is the Triple Goddess in the aspect of wise elder. She is deeply magical, full of wisdom and secrets. She retains the curiosity and inquisitiveness of the Maiden, the loving nature of the Mother, but as Crone, has gained mastery over the magical arts. She teaches us that the end of life is simply the pause before the circle continues: death precedes rebirth, and so the Wheel continues.

The Crone is as mighty as the other aspects, but in her own way. She uses knowledge to enhance Her power. When she teaches, her lessons may be more stern than the other faces of the Triple Goddess, but they are just as loving. The Crone guards the secrets of prophecy; this is two-fold. She has seen all that life can give and so can easily predict the future based on the information presented to her in the present; she also knows the ancient divining ways, and is happy to gift these to younger generations.

The Crone keeps to Herself in her studies, and so to connect with Her, you need to go calling for Her. Like Baba Yaga in her chicken-legged hut in the forest, the Crone sits and waits, absorbed in the magic of the universe, until the grandchildren come knocking for treats and lessons.

Some of the many goddesses who embody the aspect of the Crone are: Baba Yaga, Badb, Ceridwen, Elli, Hecate, Kali, Lara, Macha, The Morrigan, Nepthys, and Oya.

The Sun God

In Wiccan and pagan traditions, and in faiths and religions across the world and from the beginning of humanity, the Sun has been worshipped as the Giver of Life and the most holy of deities known to Earth. Without the Sun, there would be no life here.

The God worshipped in his role of the Sun is observed throughout the Wiccan Wheel of the Year. At Yule in December he is reborn, and so we are given hope during the shortest day and the longest night that soon, there will be less darkness in the world. At Beltane, the Sun has just reached adulthood, and His youthful spirit and enthusiasm is evident in the raucous, rowdy Maypole dances and bonfires. At Midsummer, the Sun has reached His pinnacle of power, and we bask in his loving rays until Harvest comes at Lammas, where He lays his own body down into the fields to give us the very last nourishment of the year.

Some of the many gods who embody the aspect of the Sun God are: Apollo, Balder, Freyr, Garuda, Helios, Lugh, Ra, and Surya.

The Oak King and the Holly King

The Oak King represents the brighter, warmer half of the Wheel of the Year, when we are nearer the sun and its life-giving rays. The Oak King is born at Yule, grows in strength during the rest of Winter and early Spring, then becomes a virile young man at Beltane, finally to assume the height of His power, seated at the Midsummer throne during Litha. By the time Harvest comes at Lammas, He is in decline. By Samhain, the Oak King has passed.

The Oak King represents warmth, passion, direct action, and confidence. He is physicality and prowess, the steady arrow shot from the hunter's bow. He represents male virility and the power of creation.

The Holly King represents the darker six months of the Wheel of the Year. He is born during the bonfires of Midsummer, and ascends the throne as His counterpart rescinds it. The Holly King rises to power during the darkening days and hours of the harvest, of Samhain when the veil between the worlds is the most thin, coming to His full potential soon after. At Yuletide He rules with all of His power for one brief night, then passes on as the Sun begins to make its way back from the darkness.

The Holly King represents subtly and the wisdom of the trickster. He is cold and logical, physically sly as the fox, a keen blade wielded in the dark. He represents wisdom, secrets and the power of the storyteller.

The Green Man

The Green Man, also known as Herne, originated in Britain and is connected with the woodlands and the fields. He is a shepherd of beasts, keeping a watchful eye on the animals of the wilderness. The Green Man is often depicted as having a wild, unkempt crown and beard of vines and leaves. You can still see images of Him in ancient churches throughout the United Kingdom today. The Green Man and the following Horned God are often viewed as the same deity.

The Horned God

Also known as Cernunnos, the Horned God is one of the oldest and most recognizable gods featured in Wicca and other pagan faiths; with a head of stag's horns, the mysterious Horned God is both the Hunter and the Keeper of the forest. He is united with the Mother goddess in symbolic fertility rites to celebrate the abundance of the land and the fields. Many consider Him to be the male equivalent of the Triple Goddess, as He rules over birth, life, and death as well as the afterlife.

Some of the many gods who embody the aspect of the Horned God are: Herne the Hunter, Janus, Pan, Osiris, Dionysus, and the Green Man.

Deciding Whether Or Not to Incorporate a Deity Into Your Faith

It is up to the Wiccan as to whether they decide to reach out and connect with a deity or deities as part of their spiritual path. It is not required. Many find that they need to work out feelings about authority figures or parental roles before they can begin to forge a relationship with an otherworldly being.

Some things to consider when deciding this is that, unlike Judeo-Christian or Abrahamic faiths, Wicca does not hold that we are *subservient* to the God and Goddess—also referred to as the Lord and Lady. We are their children, and loved by Them. Sometimes we may have our own issues to work out regarding our mothers and fathers. That is normal and natural. Some Wiccans prefer to view the gods as teachers, masters to our apprentice role, wise and patient, ready and willing to hear about our fears and misgivings.

Still others turn to the gods as peers and friends. None of this is disrespectful. Intention is everything, and if you choose to approach and reach out to a god or goddess, know that your intention and your heart will be read by Them fairly and with reciprocated love. We honor Them by speaking to Them; we contribute to the pulse of Their spirit with our own. While not ever deity teaches lessons the same way—some may be playful and fun, others healing and infinitely patient, still others may be quiet and stern—they all have ancient wisdom to share, and they are happy to share it.

If you decide to walk the path of nature alone, and prefer not to connect with a god or goddess, that is *completely acceptable*. Some Wiccans devote a section of their altar to their ancestors and beloved dead. And some merely seek to connect with nature.

Nature Spirits

There are many Earthly religions that worship nature spirits, such as the Japanese Shinto. A Wiccan following this path will revere the inner spirit of every aspect of the natural world, from herbs to oaks, animals to fish, birds and insects, weather patterns and moons.

We can worship and connect with nature spirits by learning the symbolism of living things in regards to that spirit. For instance, the herb basil is connected to the Element of fire, and is used in money and fertility magic. Making an offering of fresh basil to the Fire elemental spirits would go well with a spell cast for good luck in money and finances.

Chapter 4: The Wheel of the Year

Wiccan Sabbaths

Because Wicca has no single, central holy book or text, such as the Christian bible, Jewish torah or Muslim Quran, outsiders often view Wicca as disorganized, even freeform. There is a unifying theme throughout Wicca however—its tenets and calendar may not follow a book, but the follow the changing seasons of the Earth. Wiccans call the seasonal celebrations the *sabbaths, or sabbats.*

The Wiccan year begins and ends at Samhain, the first time of year when the veil between the material world and the spirit world is at its most thin. The other time of year when the veil is thin is at Beltane, celebrated on May 1st.

Solitary Wiccans as well as those in covens and communities celebrate the sabbaths. It is perfectly acceptable to celebrate one, several, or all. Sometimes just knowing the date and observing the magic of the natural world around you is enough to feel as if you're part of something larger. There is no wrong way to mark a Sabbath— it is an opportunity for you to connect with the natural world, the God and the Goddess, and the spirits of nature in your own, unique way.

There are four Sun Festivals among the sabbaths, two are equinoxes—Ostara and Mabon, the spring and fall equinoxes, respectively. Two are solstices—Yule and Litha, the winter and summer solstices. The interesting thing about the equinox sabbaths is that magic aimed at achieving or maintaining balance is a perfect choice to be performed on these days. On the solstices, the opposite is true—either dark has domain over light, or light is the champion above dark. By focusing on the nature of every sabbath, one can draw wisdom and self-reflection, as well as imbue our magic with greater meaning.

There are also the Fire Festivals among the sabbaths, which are not related to Earth's place in orbit around the sun. These are Samhain, Imbolc, Beltane and Lammas (also known as Lughnasadh). These sabbaths occur on the same date each year, and when magic is cast during these times it is especially powerful.

In the southern hemisphere, the Wheel of the Year is a mirrored reflection of the northern hemisphere's, so Samhain occurs on May 1st, Beltane on October 31st, and so on.

Samhain – October 31st to November 1st

On Samhain, we can feel the edge of Winter moving towards us. The year is drawing down; third harvest—that of cabbages and of root vegetables—is finishing. The leaves are the colors of fire and the wind carries a mournful tone to it. Samhain is many things at once: funeral and bright, mysterious and full of light, steeped in memory and also the last warmth from Summer. We can be hopeful during Samhain that we have enough strength and inner fire within our spirits that Winter will not daunt us. Samhain is a time of storing-up, gathering close, and bolstering ourselves for the darkest season of the year.

During Samhain, the beloved dead and our ancestors are honored. Farmers used to light fires in turnips and pumpkins throughout their fields, so that lost spirits might take comfort in lit paths and find their way towards a comfortable hearth. Food and drink flow freely on Samhain, and sweets and tokens of friendship are given to raise our own spirits. Bonfires are lit on Samhain, almost to dare the darkness, and to show our might in the world. Humanity and the spirit world come together to unite forces against sorrow and pain. We are stronger together. We will not fear death, nor the dark.

At this time in the year, the Crone aspect of the Goddess rises to Her greatest power. She gathers us close to learn her wisdom and hear her stories. She shares the mystery of the fire with us, and teaches us herbal medicines. The elders of families are given honor in covens and community circles everywhere.

Samhain is pronounced " SOW-when" most commonly. It is also called Hallow's, Hallowed Eve, and All Hallows, as well as the more modern Halloween and ancient All Soul's Day. On this day, a " Mute Supper" - a plate of food set out for the spirits, is left at the table and the door to the house is opened to allow any visitors passage. On Wiccan altars, photos and notes to ancestors and beloved family members who have passed are set among traditional offerings such as apples, pomegranates, and chrysanthemum blossoms. The tradition of carving turnips for lanterns has been replaced by carving pumpkins: turnips are plants representational of the afterlife and the dead, while pumpkins are a sacred plant of the Mother goddess. The tradition has uniquely come about to symbolize life after death.

Magic and spellwork appropriate to Samhain include writing wishes on bay leaves to toss into the bonfire, focusing on looking inward for reflection, casting divination spells and reading runes or tarot cards, and envisioning what you want to accomplish in the coming new year.

Samhain's colors: crimson, pumpkin, black, gray

Suitable herbs and plants: Rosemary, rue, garlic, foxglove (poisonous), mugwort, frankincense

Foods and drink of Samhain: Roast meats, nuts, root vegetables and stuffed cabbage, savory breads, honeyed cakes, sweets and candy, meade, red wine, cider, grape juice, ale, smoked tea.

Samhain Goddesses: Aradia, Baba Yaga, Hecate, Hel, the Morrigan, Nepthyis, and Oya

Samhain Gods: Anubis, Ellegua, the Horned God, Loki, Olodumare, and Thoth

Yule – December 21st

On Yule, Wiccans's ceremonies and rituals focus on an important theme in humanity's experience: the prospect of hope. This is the shortest day and the longest night of the year. Yule is also the first sabbath of the new year, and the Winter solstice. Celebrants come together this night for community, camaraderie, and for cheer. There is special cause for celebration, you see, because this is the night when the Sun God is reborn—though merely an infant, even the faintness of His light is enough to warm our hearts. If you notice a similarity between the Christian celebration of Christmas and Jesus' birth, that is because the Roman Catholic church adopted Yuletide celebrations in the name of their Lord, so that pagan peasants would be more apt to peacefully come to the fold.

Yule is a fire festival, and as such, there is often a bonfire lit, candles glowing about the home and on the altar, and a proper " Yule log" burning in the hearth—this, too, is an originally pagan tradition syncretized by the Christian Church. Often the remnant of last year's Yule log is used to light the current year's. Other originally pagan traditions include decorating the home and altar with evergreen fronds and boughs, the decoration of a fir tree brought indoors, and a practice called " wassailing", which entails going from door to door singing songs of cheer, similar to the modern tradition of caroling.

Yule is a wonderful sabbath on which to practice gratitude. Gratitude is essential for successful, happy living—magic notwithstanding. When we adopt a mindset of gratitude, we kindle within ourselves the power to banish the darkness; we are essentially *looking on the bright side*, which is exactly what Yule is all about. Magic based to rekindle our inner spark is perfect for this time of year, as is spells to enliven creative inspiration and encourage reunion between estranged friends or family members.

Yuletide traditions can vary from community to community, and coven to coven. On this holiday, both the Crone aspect of the goddess and the newborn aspect of the God are worshipped. The day after Yule begins the Earth's journey towards Spring, so Yule is an especially happy holiday, which is why the practice of gift-giving became so popular in ancient times. The deities Santa Claus and Mother Holle hail from those ancient times, reminding us to give love and light, cheer and pleasantries that will delight the spirit and encourage our friends and families to have hope.

Magic and spellwork appropriate to Yule include dedication ceremonies, spells to rekindle lost inspiration or creativity, spells for wealth and money, and divination magic.

Yuletide colors: silver and gold, green and crimson, white

Suitable herbs and plants: Mistletoe, myrrh, pine, birch, and oak

Foods and drink of Yule: Game meat such as venison, foul, rice and wheat, root vegetables, sweet dishes, seed cakes, honey, red wine, cider, dark ale, wassail (spiced punch)

Yule Goddesses: Hera, Isis, Hel, Mother Holle

Yule Gods: Ra, Balder, Odin, Herne, Lugh, Dionysus, Bacchus

Imbolc – February 2nd

On Imbolc, the first signs of Spring are celebrated, as well as the potential for humanity to look past a bleak, and possibly bitterly-cold landscape, and see the potential still sleeping beneath the soil. This day is sacred to Brigid (pronounced *Bride)*, an Irish goddess of fire, the cauldron, blacksmithing, poetry, and creativity, and Oya, a Yoruban goddess of the marketplace, lighting, the rainbow, and the cemetery. Imbolc is also called Candlemas, and Groundhog Day is celebrated on this day as well. Crocuses may appear on Imbolc, depending on where you live—signs that the Goddess is returning from her journey to the underworld (as embodied by the goddess Persephone) and is reborn.

Imbolc focuses on life and light. It seeks to uplift the reveler with renewed joy and spirit. On this day, more fires are lit, and homes and altars are decorate with dozens of white candles. Some traditions have a young woman or girl (a bride, symbolically) wear a crown of candles to represent the Goddess in Her maiden aspect.

Wiccans look at Imbolc as a time of renewal. They will often smudge and spiritually cleanse their altars and homes to clear out any negative or stagnant energy that's built up over the Winter. As we spend more time indoors during this season, we can feel " cooped up" and run down—Imbolc refreshes us with an infusion of Maiden energy, ready to explore and create.

Imbolc was traditionally the time that the first lambs of Spring were brought into the world; farmers would celebrate the return of life to their farms. Spring flowers decorate altars and tables, and dairy dishes are served as a reminder of the ancient tradition of honoring the " Ewe's Milk".

Magic and spellwork appropriate to Imbolc include dedication, wiccaning (Wiccan naming ceremonies), blessing of magical tools, spells for new projects and creations, and spellwork to set forth a goal in motion.

Imbolc's colors: white, pale green and pale yellow, lavender

Suitable herbs and plants: crocuses and irises, forsythia, blackberries, heather

Foods and drink of Samhain: Dairy dishes, seeded bread, sweet pastries, quiche, greens, hopping John, preserves, herbal tea, white wine, pale beer, and white grape juice

Samhain Goddesses: Artemis, Brigid, Persephone and Kore, Oya

Samhain Gods: Cernunnos, Herne, Horus, Ochosi, Thor

Ostara – March 21st

On Ostara, also known as the Spring Equinox, Spring is at its height and we can finally feel the Sun's rays warming the Earth again. The forces of light and dark are in perfect balance, and we, too, may begin to feel more settled, stronger, and more even-tempered, especially if we've suffered from seasonal sadness disorder or the winter blues. The Oak King is reaching sexual maturity; at Beltane He will join with the Goddess as his equal and his mate. For now, however, the Earth is just beginning to unfurl from its Winter sleep, and we can enjoy the promise of life and beautiful things to come.

The home and the altar are decorated with indoor plants, bouquets of cut flowers, dyed and painted eggs representing the Goddess coming closer to the aspect of Mother, and woven crowns and solar crosses of sweet grass. Eggs and hares originated their symbolism with pagan roots; these, too, have been adopted in modern Christianity as symbols of the holiday of Easter. The etymology of the name Ostara comes from an ancient European goddess named " Eostre"; from Her name we have the word " estrus".

Since the days and nights are in perfect balance at Ostara, we can focus on magic to balance ourselves as well. Self healing spells, magic to enhance personal strength, achievement, and charisma, as well as peace-inducing spells, or magic to produce a beneficial outcome for all parties are particularly well-suited to this sabbath. This is not a time to crave power over something or someone, especially: we can learn a lot from the natural balance of Nature, the seasons, and the Lord and the Lady of Wicca.

Another magic spell that is particularly effective on Ostara is seed blessings magic: take seeds of whatever variety you like, and bless them beneath the Ostara moon (keeping in mind that if you're seeking something to come into fruition and the moon is either dark or waning, then the spell may remove something it deems an obstacle before you get what you desired). Then plant them in soil enriched by the Goddess's energy, and watch things unfold as the seeds germinate, and grow.

Ostara's colors: green, purple, yellow, pale blue, pink

Suitable herbs and plants: violets, lavender, chamomile, iris, hyacinth, lilies

Foods and drink of Ostara: fruit cakes, sweet pastries, egg dishes, seed and nut cakes, honey mead, champagne, fruited cider, lavender cordial, fruit tea

Ostara Goddesses: Eostre, Persephone, Saraswati, Oshun, Aphrodite, Rhiannon

Ostara Gods: Angus, Apollo, Pan, Osiris, Cupid, Zaka

Beltane – May 1ˢᵗ

Also known as May Day, Beltane is a celebration of fire, or passion, of hearts united, of the twin flames of the universe, the God and the Goddess, finally uniting as one and realizing their most fertile potential. Divine sexuality is revered on Beltane, and communities often symbolize this by the rite of placing the athame, or ceremonial blade, into the chalice, to represent the masculine merging with the feminine. For Wiccans, all sexuality is blessed, so long as it is practiced with consent.

On Beltane Eve we can feel the first shiver of Summer's warmth coming on the air; bonfires are lit to welcome the Sun back to His throne, and covens and communities will serve a wedding feast to honor the newly-wed God and Goddess. In Scotland, shirtless Wiccans—men and women alike, their bodies and faces painted blue—march through the streets carrying torches on their way to Holyrood Park and the famous castle ruins. Beltane is a time of release and passion, of excitement and pure, undiluted joy.

Another popular ritual practiced on Beltane is the dance of the maypole. Traditionally, a young oak would be hewn and decorated with ribbons; once erected, the pole would be surrounded by revelers who each took hold of the end of a ribbon. Under the priest or priestesses guidance, the revelers performed an intricate, circular dance around the pole, finally enrobing it in woven colors to celebrate the God coming into sexual maturity.

Beltane is another time of the year when the veil between the worlds is the thinnest, and it is said to be sacred to the faeries. Children conceived on Beltane Eve are thought to be especially magical, and blessed by the faerie folk. It's common for Wiccans to camp out of doors on this night, often after a community circle and party; many couples who are trying to conceive choose this night, hoping for a blessing from the gods.

Magic and spellwork appropriate to Beltane are any spells concerning fertility. Fertility can also be invoked for creative spark, good ideas in business, or anyone who must draw on inner potential to create something magical.

Beltane's colors: white, purple, green, red, and orange

Suitable herbs and plants: angelica, ash, birch, cowslip, roses, mushroom circles

Foods and drink of Beltane: Roast meats, nuts, root vegetables and stuffed cabbage, savory breads, honeyed cakes, sweets and candy, meade, red wine, cider, grape juice, ale, smoked tea.

Beltane Goddesses: Fertility goddesses, Freya, Ishtar, Isis, Yemaya, Aphrodite

Beltane Gods: Angus, Apollo, Bacchus, Chango, Herne, Lugh, Pan, Ra

Litha – June 21st

During Litha, also known as Midsummer, we celebrate the triumphant Oak King finally seated once again on His throne, Lord of all He surveys. The forest and the fields are busy with life and the crops are tall and resplendent. The life of the Goddess in Her mother aspect is evident everywhere we look: flowers bob beneath sweet, sultry winds, bees and butterflies are busy collecting life-giving nectar, young animals frolic safely within the watchful eyes of their parents, famine is far from many people's minds.

For witches who practice herbal magic, midnight on Midsummer is the optimum time to harvest them to store for the rest of the year. Bonfires are lit to bless the crops, and farmers traditionally would take a flaming brand to pass over, wand-like, their crops to ensure their optimum yield. Modern Wiccans keep a candle lit during both the day and through the night to honor the Sun God. At midnight, it is possible to reveal one's true love with divining.

This is also the night that the Oak King begins to be usurped by the Holly King—although on this night, the Holly Lord is only a babe, newly-born.

By next sabbath, Lammas, the Oak King will begin to decline, passing His body back into the Earth to sacrifice Himself in order to feed humanity. Ancient traditions saw pagans roll fiery wagon wheels through the fields—a potentially dangerous practice—so that the harvest would be especially great. Additionally, after the embers of the bonfires have cooled, farmers and shepherds would lead their flocks across the ashes to protect them from harm. A cross of ashes on one's forehead was a symbol of being blessed by the Sun God.

Midsummer magic is incredibly potent. Common practices among Wiccans include blessing ceremonial tools, charging crystals, making potions, and practicing diving magic to see what's in store for the remaining half of the year.

Magic and spellwork appropriate to Litha includes protection spells for the house or individual, as is creating magical items such as wands and staves.

Creation of any kind is particularly blessed on Litha.

Litha's colors: the colors of fire, gold, green, and white

Suitable herbs and plants: toss these herbs into the sacred bonfire for good fortune and luck: heartsease, sage, honeysuckle blossoms, vervain, sunflower heads, lavender, and branches of oak

Foods and drink of Litha: Honeyed cakes, lavender cake, fruit pies, dairy dishes, fresh fruits and vegetables from the garden, red wine, berry tea, dandelion wine, mead, golden ale, sparkling water

Litha Goddesses: Danu, Frigg, Oshun and Yemaya, Hathor, Ayida, Lakshmi

Litha Gods: The Oak King, all solar gods, Pan, Cernunnos, Chango, Herne

Lammas – August 1st

On Lammas, also known as Lughnasadh, we honor the Oak King as He begins his decline, and grieve for the god Lugh, who ritually allows himself to pass into the Earth in order to save it from being barren. This sacrifice is observed by the ritual of the First Bread. Lammas translated means " Mass of Loaves". During Lammas, we observe the intersection of Summer and Autumn, and give praise to the God and Goddess for giving us life and the wonder of a bountiful harvest.

Lammas can be a somber time for many, however. We can see the summer coming to an end as plants begin to pale and wither in the baking sun. We feel as if we want to hold onto the beautiful summer days, yet part of us longs for the cool, crisp reflection of Autumn. We may be overcome with heat and passion, and ready for more cerebral pursuits. The cooler nights of Lammas can be a great relief, promising a time that is better for introverts. The Holly King is lord of these concepts: He bades us to look inward, to gather secrets, to acquire knowledge. We sit around fires in the dark telling stories to thrill us with wonder and fear—in these moments, the Holly King is near.

Spellwork regarding thanks, abundance, wealth, prosperity, true love, and divination are good practices during the Lammas sabbath. There is usually a First Harvest feast, with plenty of freshly baked bread, as a feature of celebration. Now is also a good time to volunteer, or to give to charity, honoring and helping those who perhaps did not have a good harvest this year—metaphorically or otherwise.

Lammas' colors: gold, red, and brown, yellow and white

Suitable herbs and plants: onion, mugwort, rue, wheat, sage, thyme, oregano

Foods and drink of Lammas: loaves of bread especially wheat, dairy dishes, apple pies, pork and mutton, mulled cider, sparkling fruit juices, fruit teas, amber ale, white wine

Lammas Goddesses: Danu, Demeter, Pomona, Tailtiu, Vestia

Lammas Gods: Chronos, Dionysus, Lugh, Saturn

Mabon - 21st

This sabbath, also known as Harvest Home, is considered the second harvest of the Wheel of the Year. This is the height of harvest and of the bounty that we are given by the Lord and Lady. At this time, we may first notice the veil between the spirit and the mortal world grow thin: we may feel restless and full of energy that we don't understand, particularly during full moons. Our ancestors are beginning to reach out to us at this time, sending us guidance and wisdom. We may seek answers only the spirits can provide for us; divination is a good practice at this time, so long as we are properly shielded and grounded.

In ancient times, this is the time of year when most of the work of rural year is complete, and rest and restorative activities are under way. Mabon represents the concept of taking a well-justified break after hard work. We should relax this day, enjoying the company of family, friends, and beloved pets and animal familiars. Generously-laden tables and sweet libations are all appropriate ways to celebrate Mabon.

Both aspects of prosperity magic can be practiced on Mabon: giving thanks for good fortune, continuing good fortune and abundance, and money magic to draw riches and wealth towards us. Magic to sweeten our homes and our spirits can be performed at this time as well.

Mabon's colors: brown and gold, yellow and silver, green and orange

Suitable herbs and plants: bay leaves, juniper berries, tarragon, myrrh, mint

Foods and drink of Mabon: vegetable and fruit dishes, baked breads, dairy dishes, roasted meats, candied root vegetables, honey and fruit cakes, red wine, cider, hearty ale, fruit juice

Mabon Goddesses: Persephone, Pomona, Frigg, Hera, Rhea

Mabon Gods: Lugh, Bacchus, Obatala, Apollo, Inari (considered neither or both male and female, Inari is a Japanese agricultural deity)

Esbats and the Phases of the Moon

Esbats are celebrations and/or rites that coincide with the phases of the moon; in a sense they are a second Wheel of the Year. Most covens and communities focus on the year's full moons exclusively, but there are, in fact, many opportunities to focus one's magic, depending on the phase and cycle of the moon. Each phase is a chance to learn about a particular aspect of the human experience and the natural world.

The Triple Goddess also coincides with the three major phases of the moon: The Maiden is most powerful during the new to waxing moon phase, the Mother is at her utmost potency during the full moon, and the Crone presides over the waning to dark moon phases.

Esbats are especially helpful if you find that you are not yet ready to bring a particular god or goddess into your rituals. Honoring the moon and drawing on its energy for your spellwork is a wonderful way to become introduced to Wicca and synchronize your faith with the ebb and flow of life.

If you are interested in esbat and lunar magic, there are many free apps you can download for your phone to help you pinpoint the exact timing of the moon phases.

The Full Moon

When first learning about casting spells, it's important to realize that there is a proper time for every spell, as well as a purpose. The full moon is when energy is at its highest peak—which might lead you to believe that all spells should be performed at this time. However, the nature of the full moon is manifestation—not every spell you cast will be about receiving, or seeing something through to its culmination. Sometimes there is a need to cast spells that let things go, even destroy—such as an illness, or mental block that's hampering our courage or success.

The full moon is a good time to draw upon the Mother goddess' energy for tough challenges, and for when you feel as if your own personal power needs a lunar boost. This is why we magically " charge" our tools, potions, minerals, and other implements beneath the full moon's light; just as we charge our tablets and phones, so do our magical items need a re-charging now and again. The energies of the moon are nourishing and generous; the Goddess is there for us whenever we need Her.

Spells to perform during the Full Moon include healing spells, magic for gaining money, drawing abundance and good fortune, prosperity, success, dream magic, improving psychic abilities, and divination. We can bless and charge herbal magical recipes during this time, such as elixirs, potions, and sachet pillows. Herbs can be harvested under a full moon also for the maximum potential.

Throughout the year, there are North American names for each full moon of every month, and each moon has a different meaning:

In January, the Wolf moon means that you need to fill yourself with courage, but also that you need to keep your eyes open for opportunities and insights. Success will come but you may have to *hunt* it.

In February, the Snow moon means that you may feel as if you're hibernating; the snow blankets everything, but there is life beneath its surface. Remember to honor your subconscious as it stirs beneath the surface of your thoughts.

In March, the Worm Moon means that life is beginning to activate again. The soil is warming; there is potential for growth and change.

In April, the Pink Moon means that changes are coming; tap into this Maiden magic to spark benevolent change in your life.

In May, the Flower Moon means that the Spring is here; flowers are blooming, the air is warming, and growth and love are possible. Reach out to capture some of this uplifting energy.

In June, the Strawberry Moon means that life is full of sweetness. Perform spells of gratitude and to take part in the heady abundance that surrounds you.

In July, the Buck Moon means that the Oak King is at His highest potential, and masculine energy reaches its apex. Weather magic, spells for personal-strength, wealth, luck, and sexual energy are good to perform at this time.

In August, the Sturgeon Moon means that water magic is particularly powerful at this time. Spells for abundance, money luck, love, and healing are appropriate now.

In September, the Harvest Moon means that we are blessed with abundance and community. Reach out to friends, community, and family if you are in need of help, you will receive more than you needed. Give thanks for blessings, and if you're able, give to someone in need.

In October, the Hunter's Moon means that we can learn from the ways of the young god and Maiden goddess; take initiative, be bold, but also use your senses to observe before you act. Magic for divination is particularly helpful at this time.

In November, the Beaver Moon means that it is time to build up supplies of what we need to get us through the cold and the dark of Winter. Magic for abundance, personal happiness, healing, and joy is especially appropriate at this time.

In December, the Cold Moon means that the longest dark is nearly over; the Sun God is newly born, and we give thanks for the joy and light that exists in our lives.

The New Moon

The new moon's energy can often be unsettling for some people. It's a time that subtly reveals things we were not perhaps ready to deal with yet. However, this is a positive time, and unlike the bold and brash full moon, the new moon is more gentle and patient. We can begin magic that *builds* towards something, such as a change of attitude, healing an old, emotional hurt, finding an exciting new job, being ready for new love.

Spells to perform during the New Moon include personal-improvement, healing, job search, attracting a larger, steady income, constant abundance, and inner strength.

The Dark Moon

While some witches will not practice magic on the dark moon, it is important to realize that there is no " wrong" time to cast a spell—merely, the path on which your intent travels, and the things that may need to occur before it reaches its destination, will differ depending on when you cast your magic. The dark moon is quite frankly a time when the Crone is at Her utmost power, and She makes no bones about protecting Her children. If there is something that you absolutely must get rid of in your life—a dangerous stalker, a life-threatening illness, an addiction, an upcoming foreclosure or eviction—then this would be the right time to address that and cast magic in order to help you gain an advantage or your freedom.

The Dark Moon draws upon the wisdom of the Crone, and so advises us to " see" without our eyes, because there is no light from the moon to aid us at this time. Therefore, divination of any kind is a good practice during the dark moon. We're not using our sight to see, but our intuition and third eye.

The Waxing Moon

The waxing moon builds our energy up to culminate at the height of the full moon. If you feel that a spell needs extra steps and/or time to reach its maximum potential, then consider starting it during the waxing moon and finishing it under the full moon. Potions and candle magic are good choices for this; you can work on the recipe or light the candle at a certain time each night or day, then let the candle burn down completely or the potion steep beneath the lunar light during the full moon.

The Waning Moon

The waning moon is a time for ridding ourselves of things, or gently moving an influence away from us. It is a calmer, more easily-controlled energy than the dark moon. The dark moon is akin to Kali the Destroyer—She is a benevolent goddess who's simply very powerful, and does whatever She can to protect her followers, particularly women. The waxing moon is more like Hecate: it has patience with us as we wield our broom and sweep the negative aspect or energy from our hearts, minds, and homes. A change in diet or exercise for better health can be performed beneath the waning moon, or any spell that requires us to slowly come around to the idea of something, rather than abruptly and suddenly.

Days of the Week

If you want to really zero in on a specific purpose or intent with your spellcasting, try picking a certain day of the week to boost its efficacy.

Sunday is the day of the Sun, and an all-around beneficial day for magic that brings about positive change or growth. Therefore it's best-suited for spellcasting relating to money magic, wealth, increasing a good reputation, healing, strengthening, and bringing joy to one's heart. Magic for successful job searches or to ensure your work is excellently-crafted is also fitting for this day.

Monday is the day of the Moon. While magic cast on this day may be uncertain, or even slow-moving, it is still a beautifully magical day, and good for working with divination, dreams, as well as exploring our emotions and performing fertility spells. Women especially can benefit from meditation and wellness magic on Mondays.

Tuesday is the day of Mars. Do your best not to wear red on this day to avoid attracting conflict, however, if you want the advantage in a struggle or challenge, slip a red stone in your pocket or wear a small bit of red hidden, such as a woven bracelet. Today is an excellent day for protection and strength magic, as well as bolstering one's courage.

Wednesday is Mercury's day, the God of communication. Mercury also rules change, protects the artist, and is in charge of fun and games. The Yoruban god Ellegua is another version of Mercury; he carries around a sack full of toys and also is the messenger between all of the other gods, and he rules the crossroads. Wearing red on Wednesday will bring you good luck, especially against an adversary. Using ferns in herbal magic will give them a great boost on a Wednesday. Perform spells for creative inspiration, to hear good news, to make sure your messages reach their intended target with speed and efficacy, and to boost your luck with money and wealth.

Thursday is Jupiter's day, the god of expansion, good fortune, prosperity, and abundance. Thursday is also named after Thor, the Nordic god known for his strength and generosity. On Thursday, perform spells to bring good health and wealth. The colors for this day are dark purple and deep blue: perform a candle spell for good fortune, and add a cup of red wine or grape juice for Jupiter or Thor if you like to bless your magic.

Friday is Venus' day, and also belongs to other goddesses of love and unbridled desire such as Oshun and Oya. It is a good day to perform love and beauty magic, as well as magic to attract customers if you are self-employed or own your own business. It is a day that favors the bold innovator of the marketplace. You can also perform rites to boost self-esteem, and heal from wounds of the heart.

Saturday is Saturn's day. It is an excellent day for performing any protection and banishment magic. It's also a good day to spiritually cleanse yourself or your home. Use sage, palo santo wood, or rosemary to burn and " smudge" your ritual space or room clean, then follow with sweet incense or a white candle.

Chapter 5: The Magic of Wicca

Many people think that magic is something that is beyond them, or that they need years of training to master it. Like any other art that you love, you will find the longer you practice witchcraft, the better you become at it—but that's only because the meanings and significances of what goes into your spell will become rote, memorized, and second nature. You're inherent *energy* that you'll use to cast the spell is already there inside you. Your intent is also already there. All you have to do in order to be successful at magic is to make the decision to cast it.

Many of us have been drawn to magic and the natural world all of our lives. Perhaps as a child, you had a favorite " rock and stick" collection. These are indications that you were curious about the energy inherent in objects, and felt it was important to utilize this energy in some way. Many young children cause their parents to chuckle when they find them with a bowl of water and wildflowers they've collected. Children's intuitions are often far better at tuning into the rhythms and flow of nature, as their brain waves operate on a deeper level until they reach puberty. This natural curiosity and ability to sense the energy all around us never goes away, however. Magic is part of the natural world, and it's ours to use, if we choose to.

What we have learned throughout the years is that magic, like any other force of nature, does better when it's controlled. So, how do you control it? This is where the wisdom of our elders comes in. The following chapter goes over all the ways you can control your magic and put it to use in the form of a magical spell.

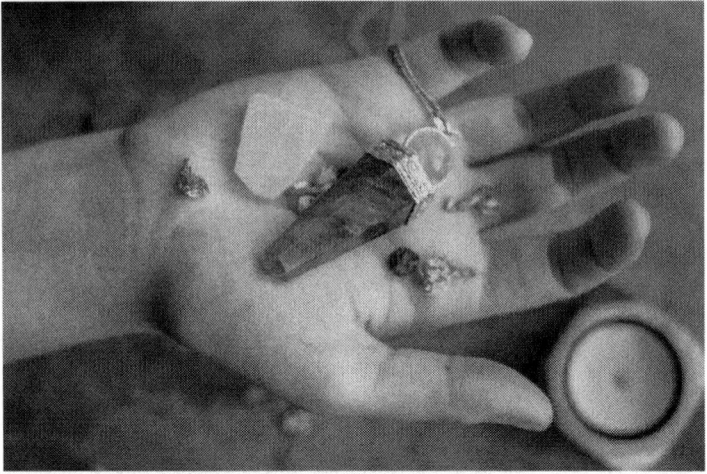

Preparing Yourself For Magic

Any experienced Wiccan will admit that they've
performed magic " on the fly", and that's
perfectly acceptable. But for a beginner just
starting out, it's best to go by the rule-book, so to
speak. Before you use your energy to cast a spell,
it's best to spiritually cleanse yourself, so that you
don't track any residual energy from the outside
world into your circle. Before you spiritually
cleanse, always remember to be physically clean

first. So take a shower before a spiritual bath, or wash up first before smudging, etc.

You can spiritually cleanse yourself by " smudging", or using sacred smoke to drive the negative energy from your body and your spirit. Light a bundle of sage, palo santo wood, or rosemary and lavender, and move the smoking bundle in counterclockwise circles (this direction is called *widdershins* by pagans) from the top of your head to your feet, also smudging your arms and hands.

Another way of spiritually cleansing yourself is to mix a little pink or kosher salt into your bathwater, or in your body wash if you choose to shower instead. Cleanse from head to feet, moving in widdershins circles. When you dry off, also dry off from head to toe.

Make sure all of your spell ingredients and magical tools are placed at your altar, as well as any mundane items you will need, such as paper and pencil, matches, candleholders, small dishes or bowls, etc.

The Elements

When we talk about the elements, obviously we are not referencing those that are found on the periodic table. For thousands of years, humanity has observed different types of magical energy inherent in matter and life on Earth. When we discuss the Elements, its the nature of these energies that we are referring to.

Earth

Earth is represented by the direction of the North. Earth is the ground upon which we stand; it lends foundation to all of our endeavors, including our most important endeavor: our life. The Earth is a constantly-changing canvas of birth, growth, death, and rebirth. It is the mountains as well as the desert, the rich plains and the forests. The Hunter God and the Goddess of Agriculture are represented by the Earth element. The Earth represents logic, knowledge, steadfastness, sturdiness. Earth is powerful in an ancient, long-lasting, and quiet way. It takes a lot to move Earth.

Earth has a unique connection to Water; Water activates Earth but can also overcome it, as seen in the case of rivers carving out canyons from sheer rock. Water represents emotion, especially, and emotion can move the unmovable.

Earth as an element represents stability, wealth, riches, and abundance. This element also symbolizes the Mother goddess and the divine womb, shelter, divination, craftspeople and farmers, and the blacksmith. Gods and goddesses of Earth include Gaia, the Horned God, Herne,

Ogun, Ochosi, and Pan. The colors of Earth are black, brown, green, and gray. Crystals imbued with Earth energy are agate, jade, mica, onyx, and chrysoprase. The seasons connected to Earth is Winter.

The Earth astrological signs are Taurus, Virgo, and Capricorn. Earth people love home and family; they are also very sensual. They love their tables full and their beds comfortable. They treat their partners with deep attention. Romantically elegant, Earth people love the finer things in life.

Air

Air is the swiftest element, connecting every living thing on the planet through the necessary life-force of breath and oxygen. Air is invisible, and yet its effects are instantly visible: Air is the wind, the tornado, and the dust-devil. It is the force that drives usually-calm Water to destruction in the form of a hurricane. Air brings pollen on currents of dust from the African desserts to the South American rain forests. Air is language, intelligence, insight, and wit. Unlike Earth, Air is not fixed; it is the cause of rapid change, but it can also be gentle, like a warm breeze in Summer.

Air has a unique connection to Fire. It gives Fire life and can also stir Fire to cause destruction. Many things that are created in Fire, such as steel, require Air in order to be forged as well. Air is ethereal; it represents the direction of the East.

Air as an element represents communication and connection. Air is active wherever people come together to discuss things, or travel to new places; the elemental energy of Air is present in libraries, places of education, bus terminals and airports, as well as newsrooms and traffic control towers. Gods and goddesses of Air include: Ellegua, Shu, Thoth, Mercury, Coyote, and Athena. The colors of Air are white, silver, blue, and gray. Crystals imbued with Air energy are herkimer diamond, white quartz, laboradorite, smoky quartz and pink quartz. The seasons connected to Air is Spring.

The Air astrological signs are Aquarius, Gemini, and Libra. Air people love to engage in debate and analyze situations. They opt for logic over emotion, and love to exchange ideas and theories. Air people can be impulsive, never putting roots down for too long, and lovers may find them too engrossed in fantasy and other realms to ever connect deeply.

Fire

Fire is a popular element because it is so obviously, visually *magical.* It captures the attention of the witch because it embodies things that make life delightful: heat, warmth, beauty. And yet, fire directly harms life when touched. It isn't necessary for life, and yet it makes life enjoyable. Fire is a paradox, and yet its divinity is proven in the fact that the stars and the Sun are made of it. Light is a life-giver, and without we would not exist. The Element of Fire is associated with passion, desire, sparks of genius, creativity, health, and strength. Fire can temper and create, but it can also damage and destroy. Because it impacts the human spirit so strongly, Fire is an essential component in most rituals and sabbath-related rites.

Fire has a unique connection with Earth, in that when the two are combined, radical change occurs. Metal is ruled by Earth, and when super-heated becomes a powerful sword or cunning knife. Forests exist that can only spread their seeds when a wild-fire runs freely through them. Fire bakes mud into materials that provide shelter.

Fire as an element represents innovation, motivation, the force of will, and courage. The element of Fire is connected with the South. Gods and goddesses of Fire include Apollo, Lugh, Ra, Sekhmet and Pele. The colors of Fire are red, orange, white, and black. Crystals imbued with Fire energy are opal, tiger's eye, garnet, and ruby. The season connected to Fire is Summer.

The Fire astrological signs are Aries, Leo, and Sagittarius. Fire people are loyal but also desire revenge when wronged. They are quick to begin new things. Their emotions change quickly, but when the love, they love with passion. Fire people are innovators and love anything that's new and bold. They enjoy attention and often love to be recognized for their traits—both good and bad.

Water

Water is the deepest element, connected to memory, the dream-world, emotions and the subconscious mind. It presides over our hearts, and promotes healing, empathy, and understanding. Without Water, we would perish. It is life-giving and the Earth's greatest resource. The nature of Water is fluid and never fixed, even when frozen. From Water we create medicine, and enable the land to grow crops for our Harvest table. The human body is made up of 80% water, and water sustains us even in the womb. The element of Water is sacred to the Goddess and its nature is feminine.

Water has a unique connection to the Earth. The Earth grounds Water and gives it a purpose, while Water enriches the Earth with life.

Water as an element represents intuition and ancestral connection, the powers of emotion, medicine and healing, childbirth and creativity, and empathy. The element of Water is connected to the West. Gods and goddesses of Water include Neptune, Oshun, Yemaya, Venus, and Tiamat. The colors of Water are blue, indigo, white, silver, lavender, purple, green, and dark blue. Crystals imbued with Water energy are amethyst, aquamarine, peridot, hematite, pearl, and sapphire. The season connected to Water is Autumn.

The Water astrological signs are Pisces, Cancer, and Scorpio. Water people feel deeply, making lifelong connections. When they are hurt, they either retreat into their shells or lash out with surprising accuracy. Water people feel the entire world's emotions; their empathy cannot be matched. They are often a wellspring of creative power. Many writers, painters, dancers, and poets are Water signs.

Spirit

Spirit is the fifth element, and it represents humanity and its role in the casting of magic.

Without spirit, magic would simply not be. Humanity is gifted and blessed with a unique perspective—understanding one's role in the world. With that perspective comes great responsibility. The element of Spirit allows us to have both the humility to understand that the God, Goddess, and natural world are our connections and our teachers, as well as the courage to step out into that world and ford our unique paths as pioneers, explorers, observers, and innovators. It takes boldness and daring to choose to practice witchcraft. Spirit lights the spark within us that causes us to proclaim: " I am a witch! I am a Wiccan!"

Spirit exists within all of the four other elements, and so it exists in us. When we work with the elements, we are automatically linked to them by the cooperation of spirit. Spirit is the divine essence that exists in all things; the invisible weave that allows us to feel the vibration of the universe around us. Because of spirit, we are able to connect with the other elements, with the natural world, and with the divinity of the God and the Goddess. It is not easy to become aware of spirit; it usually takes some effort and practice, though some are born with a knack for sensing it.

There is no associated color, season, or direction to Spirit. The color white may be considered to be symbolic of spirit, and the pentacle representative of this element since it combines all five.

Spirit has been recognized and pondered for thousands of years. The ancient Greeks coined the term " aether" to describe the invisible, intangible essence of magic, life, and energy. Aether, roughly translated, means " higher air", and that is what the Greek philosophers first thought Spirit was. Today, many Wiccans refer to the element of Spirit as Aether. Another word, " Akasha" was coined by Hindi philosophers and priests, and is Sanskrit for " space". While this may make us think of the universe and planets, the Hindu concept of space was the invisible material that connected all things.

Regardless of how it's defined, the idea of Spirit can seem confusing and elusive, but at the same time, we instinctively *know* that it exists when we look at the stars on a summer night, or feel the wind move through the trees as we walk through the forest. It lights a fire within our souls and makes us feel wordless, undefinable connections to all life.

Regular meditation is one way to further unlock our feelings about Spirit. Great masters and teachers have promoted meditation for centuries, understanding that when we stop observing, and just simply *feel*, we become part of the fabric that is Spirit.

Casting a Circle

You don't have to cast a spell in a formal environment if you don't want to or aren't able to, and this is one of the beautiful things about Wicca. You can cast a spell in a clearing in the woods, or on a mountaintop; you can cast magic in your bedroom or your garden. Wherever you choose to cast your spell, however, you'll first need to do what's called " casting a circle". The reason we do this is to " wall-off" a small area of the universe—literally just a circle of space around us—so that we can focus our energy in that one, small space. If we didn't cast a circle, then our energy would simply spill out into the world and mingle with all of the other energy out there, instead of into our spell.

When covens and communities perform large rites and rituals, the circle that is cast is often very large, and the priest or priestess asks volunteers to call the quarters (the four elements and directions) rather than walking the entire circle themselves. As the corners are called, the entire congregation turns to face each direction and call to it in kind. It is a very powerful, moving experience to be a part of this, and one that every witch should experience at least once.

Once a circle is cast, it is best that no one enter or leave it until the spellwork and rituals are finished, and the circle is formally " opened". If you find that you must leave it, take your wand, athame (ritual knife), or your index finger, and imagine you are " cutting" a circle in the field of energy. Draw a small circle going widdershins, then step through—turn around and replace the cut circle by drawing back the missing space in a *sunwise* (clockwise) movement. When you return to the circle, complete this action to go back inside and resume your work.

Calling the Quarters

When we cast a circle, we do so by calling the quarters. The " quarters" are the four elemental directions. We give the circle physical domain by marking each direction, and also inviting the Guardians of each direction to join us for strength and protection.

Your altar or work area (if you're out of doors or working on the floor) should be facing North. If you're not sure where North is, check out your location on Google Maps or Google Earth, or download a compass app. Of just buy a physical compass from the sports section of your local super store; keep it with your magical tools, it will always come in handy.

Beginning with the North, you may use your athame, wand, or simply point with your index finger and say:

" Hail, Guardians of the North, where mountains keep safe the Earth's knowledge, join us in this humble circle, and keep us strong and safe!"

Turn sunwise (clockwise) one position to the right and face the East, and say:

" Hail, Guardians of the East, the swift wind and climbing sunrise, join us in this humble circle, and keep us imaginative and thoughtufl!"

Turn sunwise one position to the right and face the South, and say:

" Hail, Guardians of the South, where are passions' fires burns, join us in this humble circle, and keep us filled with courage and desire!"

Turn sunwise one position to the right and face the West, and say:

" Hail, Guardians of the West, where oceans run deep with emotion and memory, join us in this humble circle, and keep us filled with empathy and love!"

Standing again facing the North, say, " This circle is cast. All who join may do so in perfect love, and perfect trust."

Drawing On the Power of the Moon

After we cast a circle, we will need to fill it, or " charge" it, with energy. We bring our own energy to the circle, but why stop there? The universe is at the ready with its own energy to give us, limitless and infinite. The God and the Goddess are always there for their children, ready to help.

Most witches draw power from the moon, but you can use this exercise to ask for power from any god or goddess, another planet, or the Sun. The technique is quite simple:

Sit, kneel, or stand in your circle (sitting is recommended as drawing down the power can sometimes have the side-effect of making some people dizzy). You can raise your arms, or rest your hands, palm side up, on your legs. Close your eyes. Imagine the power of the Moon shining directly onto your circle. Ask it with your heart to join your humble circle and raise the energy within. Now imagine the Moon's energy pouring into your circle like water pouring into a well, swirling all around you in bright, shining light, spiraling up the walls, filling ever higher, until at last it reaches the top. Your circle is full. Imagine the light glowing brightly, as bright as it can be, then open your eyes. The circle is cast and charged, and you are ready to cast your spell.

Magic Needs a Purpose

When casting a spell, it's important to be as specific as possible with your intentions. Casting a spell without a direct purpose would be like sending a carrier pigeon with a note to a continent, or casting a message in a bottle into the sea. *Know* what you're asking for or planning to do before you do it.

In addition, make sure you choose the right lunar phase and day of the week for your spell, otherwise you might have results you did not expect.

Finally, *believe* in yourself. You may have had low self-confidence your whole life, or consider yourself introverted or shy, but these things do not matter here, and now. This is your right, as a witch. You have every right to use the divine energy within you to make changes in your life and your world. So first, give yourself *permission* to use the tools you have at hand—the tool of *magic*. Next, allow yourself to *dare*, to be bold, to be free! You are a witch, you will cast magic when you decide to.

Finalizing Spells

Regarding the Wiccan Rede, the Rule of Three, and casting spells—it's essential that every spell end with the Words of Casting, so that they do not cause harm while manifesting the intention and purpose you charged them with. The Words of Casting go as follows, and are to be spoken at the end of every spell:

" By the power of three times three, I cast this spell, perfectly. To harm no one nor to bring harm to me, I cast this spell, so mote it be!"

Once you've completed a spell and spoken the Words of Casting, imagine the spell as a divine rubber band, shot out into the stars, into the universe. It is set in motion now. Rest assured the results will follow.

If you choose to, record your thoughts and feelings, as well as the steps you took while casting, about this spell in your grimoire or Book of Shadows.

Opening a Circle

After you have finished your spellwork, rite, or ritual, you must open the circle (when you are ready.)

Stand at the North and say:

" Hail, Guardians of the North, thank you for your presence and protection, go with perfect love and trust!"

Turn sunwise (clockwise) one position to the right and face the East, and say:

" Hail, Guardians of the East, thank you for your presence and protection, go with perfect love and trust!"

Turn sunwise one position to the right and face the South, and say:

" Hail, Guardians of the South, where are passions' fires burns, join us in this humble circle, and keep us filled with courage and desire!"thank you for your presence and protection, go with perfect love and trust!"

Turn sunwise one position to the right and face the West, and say:

" Hail, Guardians of the West, thank you for your presence and protection, go with perfect love and trust!"

Standing again facing the North, say, " This circle is open, this circle is unbroken. Merry meet, part, and meet again."

The Importance of Grounding

After we've opened the circle and finished all of our work, grounding is an essential next step. You've both called down and raised a lot of energy while casting your spell, and without purposefully returning it to the Earth, it will remain in your body, and can cause sleeplessness, agitation, and chaotic thoughts and emotions. Simply kneel on the floor or ground, palms down, and take a deep breath; picture all of the energy from your circle flowing out of the area and into the floor or ground, down into the Earth, as water drains from a pool. Remain this way until you feel all of the extra energy you called down has been given back to the Goddess.

After spellwork, it is also important to have something to drink and eat. In covens and community rituals, this is referred to as " cakes and wine" or " cakes and ale", but any snack and beverage is acceptable. There are many community circles that prefer to keep things alcohol-free during the sabbaths.

Magical Tools, and the Wiccan Altar

As stated earlier in the book, the only " tool" the practicing witch requires is her mind. That being said, ritual, magical tools are a lovely way to help us focus our energy and keep connected with the ancestors, as well as generations of witches before us. A tool is merely an invention that helps us get the job done, so don't feel as if you're needlessly spending money if you choose to buy a magical tool. These items become treasured possessions as the years go by, and can be passed lovingly down to future generations.

You may find yourself drawn to one or more tools but not the others; this is perfectly acceptable. Some witches love to craft their own wands from found sticks; others prefer to use the athame to call the quarters and cast spells. Still others adore the cauldron, and mortar and pestle, as well as the sharp boline, as they prefer to cast their magic in the kitchen using more mundane equipment. There is no wrong way to go about collecting and acquiring magical tools.

The Altar

There are as many interpretations of the Wiccan altar as there are Wiccans. There are hand-carved and custom built altars for sale on the market and at pagan magical supply shops, but you may also use a footstool, side table, or bookshelf for your altar. Some witches keep a small altar out of the way of prying eyes, and bring it out of a closet or chest only when it's time to perform a ritual or cast a spell.

When performing magic out of doors, a beautiful choice for an altar is to use a tree stump or large rock, or a sandy spot near a river. If using natural materials, make sure you don't spill anything that could be toxic to wildlife, such as essential oil, or leave candle wax drippings or any other refuse behind.

The standard way of setting up an altar goes as such:

IMAGE OR STATUE OF THE GOD (left) OR STATUE OF THE GODDESS (right)	**IMAGE**
(a candle in the color of the God) (a candle in the color of the Goddess)	**CUP**
Magical tools: **Magical tools:**	**PENTACLE**
(athame, wand, censer, boline)	**(cauldron, mortar and pestle, bowl of water)**

Other Altar Styles to Try

Other ways to decorate your altar are limitless, and you can use your imagination to come up with your own style. Here are a few different themes to try:

White Light Altar. Decorate your altar with a white altar cloth, central white pillar candle for divine energy, and add silver bowls for salt and water, white flowers, and a mirror to sit behind the candle. Add two smaller white candles on either side to represent the Lord and the Lady, the masculine and the feminine, then four tealights to represent the four Quarters. This altar can be helpful when you need to renew the hope in your heart, refresh your spirit, or drive away sadness.

Animal Spirit Altar. Decorate your altar with a woven grass or bamboo mat (or fur, if you are not vegan and have found a pelt in a thrift store or can get one from a friend who hunts). Add symbols or statues of animals you feel drawn to. Add candles in the four Quarters in the colors of brown for North, gray for East, orange or red for the South, and green or black for the West. Use this altar to rekindle your own spirit energy, or for magic regarding pets, or for building courage.

Faerie Altar. A beautiful altar to try in the Spring and Summer months. Use a light green altar cloth. Find a picture or statue that kindles images of the faerie world in your heart, place it beside the candle for the North. Include any statues or images of creatures that align with the faerie world, such as dragonflies, foxes, snakes, beetles, and birds. For the North, choose a black or indigo-hued candle. For the East, a white candle, and for the South, a berry-colored or orange candle. Finally for the West choose a violet or lavender colored candle. Decorate further with gathered honeysuckle vines, roses, wildflowers, acorns, and feathers. Use this altar to connect to the divine wild-spirit of the Forest.

Ancestor Altar. This is a suitable altar for Samhain and Yule. Using a rich red or black altar cloth (or white, which is also appropriate as it makes us think of heaven), decorate the altar with photos, cards or letters of our beloved departed relatives. Add small items they might have enjoyed before passing, such as cigars, knitting needles, statues of dogs, toys, a hair comb. Add mixed candles about the altar, and white candles. Burn incense and leave a plate of delicious food and a glass of ice water, as well as a favorite beverage. Take your time in speaking with the ancestors; they enjoy your visits.

If you do not know your ancestors (if you were adopted, for instance) there is no reason you cannot have your own ancestor altar. It may take you some time to picture what they would like, so practice some divining: use tarot cards, runes, or simply meditate and record your thoughts in your grimoire. When you are ready, decorate your altar as if someone you are very fond of is coming to visit. You can and should also incorporate images and items from any family members of your adoptive family who have passed on.

with gathered honeysuckle vines, roses, wildflowers, acorns, and feathers. Use this altar to connect to the divine wild-spirit of the Forest.

The Athame

The athame, traditionally, is a double-edged, black handled knife. It's meant to be the metaphorical blade, used to spiritually cut things, carve symbols in the air, cast a circle, and direct power into a spell. It doesn't need to be sharp as it's only meant as a spiritual tool, unlike the boline knife which is a practical one. The athame is associated with masculine energy and the God— this of course does not mean that only masculine persons may use it. Everything has an energy and a connection—even the plants and herbs we use in spells. When it is said that something is " masculine" in nature, it speaks of its similarities to the energy of the God. Sometimes the God is direct, and of action, other times He is subtle and subversive. The athame is a tool of *direction*. It is associated with air, but is also connected to fire by some interpretations. It is linked to the minor arcana of Swords in the Tarot.

The appearance of your athame is completely up to you. If you are more the traditional type, then the black-handled, silver-bladed athame can be found in many pagan supply shops as well as online marketplaces. If you are interested in something different, you'll be able to find hand-carved, wooden athames, ceramic athames, even athames hewn from rock and crystal. Some Wiccans prefer to bless and charge an old kitchen knife and use that as an athame. The choice of which tools you use, where you acquire them, and how you use them is completely up to you.

Finding an old, wooden-handled knife at a thrift store allows you to carve your own symbols into the handle, making a wonderfully personalized handle. (Carve with caution; wrap up the blade first.)

What you should not use an athame for, traditionally, is cutting mundane things. This practice also has changed recently, and more Wiccans are choosing to use their athame to harvest herbs, carve symbols into candles for candle spells, or even carving a wand from found branches. Wiccans who self-describe as " kitchen witches", and who prepare their magic in the foods, potions, and beverages they make, often use their athame in basic food-prep. Many however still prefer to use the white-handled boline for these tasks.

When you choose your athame, it can be an advantage to have a local pagan supply or magical store close by, so that you can hold the athame and get a feel for its energy. Don't be afraid to keep looking until you've found the " one".

The Cauldron

The cauldron is certainly one of the most easily recognizable tools of the witch, carried over from actual history where the village wise woman was the herbalist, the healer, the cook, the provider of nourishment. When witches began to be maligned by modern practitioners of medicine, the cauldron was made infamous by skewed portrayal in television and film. Today with the resurgence of Wicca and other pagan faiths, the cauldron is being revisited and revered, as it rightly should be. While it's out of most budget's means to purchase a life-size, traditional cauldron, many pagan magical supply shops sell small, palm-sized or cooking pot scale cauldrons, perfect for placement on the altar or as a prized possession of the kitchen witch.

The cauldron represents the divine forces and purposes of both the Mother goddess and the Crone goddess. From the cauldron comes food, medicine, as well as creation, symbolically. As an alchemical symbol, the cauldron combines ingredients with heat to produce something that is transformed. Even the bowl-shaped curves of the cauldron are reminiscent of the potency and fertility of the Goddess. The cauldron is connected to both of the elements of Fire and Water. While the cauldron is not considered one of the " primary" tools of the Wiccan altar, it can be useful in herbal magic as well as divining. It is also quite pleasing to the eye and to the hand, so if you have an opportunity to acquire one, do!

Cauldrons are still traditionally wrought from cast iron, although ceramic, stainless steel, and copper varieties exist. If you cannot afford a cauldron or simply aren't interested in purchasing one, a black or white ceramic bowl can double as a symbolic cauldron for use in divination and herbal spells.

Other uses for the cauldron include burning incense or dried herbs. Make sure to purchase a package of charcoal " discs" from a magical supply shop, once lit, these provide a small, heated surface on which to burn loose incense or herbs.

The Chalice

The chalice is also called the goblet, or more simply, the cup. It is representative of the Element of Water, and symbolizes the fertility of the Goddess as well as creativity, wealth, and abundance. During ritual ceremony, the chalice is used to pour a libation (an offering to the Earth) on the ground. It can also be used simply on the altar to " catch" the overflow of spiritual energy when calling down the Moon, the Sun, or the power of the God and the Goddess. The traditional chalice is silver, or pewter. When choosing a chalice, make sure that if you intend to ever drink from it that is labeled " food safe". A chalice does not need to be expensive to be worthy of purchase. Any material, such as wood, glass, ceramic, stone, or silver can be used to create a chalice. The chalice is perhaps the easiest magical tool to find in a thrift store. Just look for an interesting goblet-shaped cup and see how the energy feels in your hand. Of course, you should always ritually-cleanse or smudge your new tools when you first bring them home, especially if they're purchased from a second hand shop. Even new tools have been handled by many other people, who've left an imprint of their own energy on the item, so when in doubt, always smudge and spiritually cleanse.

The chalice is connected to the suit of Cups in the Tarot.

The Pentacle

The pentacle is any disc-shaped object that has the symbol of the pentagram on it. It is the symbol of the Wiccan faith, and is inscribed on everything from necklaces to altar clothes. The pentagram represents all of the elements: Earth, Air, Fire, Water, and Spirit. Because the pentacle is round and encompasses everything on Earth, it is connected to the Goddess.

The pentagram is a symbol of both protection as well as wisdom, and arcane knowledge, which is why it's often inscribed on the covers of Grimoires, also known as Books of Shadows. Wands, athames, and amulets are often inscribed with this symbol as well. When worn, the pentacle protects the wearer from negative energy and misfortune.

Pentacles are often inscribed with other runes and symbols for further meaning, so when purchasing one, make sure that you understand what everything else on it means, or else you might accidentally acquire something that goes against your personal vision or beliefs.

The Wand

The wand is more iconic to magic than any other implement. Throughout the world's cultures, magicians, witches, sorcerers and wizards are depicted casting spells with a wand. The wand is a highly-useful tool: it may cast and open a circle, draw energy from the heavens, and call both the God and the Goddess. Because the wand is a tool of direction and shaped linearly, it is associated with the God. It is considered aligned with the Element of Air for some, but is more commonly connected to the Element of Fire, as well as the suit of Wands in the Tarot.

A wand should typically be as long as your forearm, or shorter. Wands range from the extremely decorative to the very simple and plain. They can be set with gems and bands of silver, or carved from the found branches of a tree and smoothed to perfection. There are many trees sacred to the God that lend themselves to wand-making, these are: willow, oak, elder, hazel, apple, and yew. Bamboo also, surprisingly, makes an excellent wand: it is a symbol of both luck and ingenuity, as well as perseverance, flexibility and strength. It is hollow, so small runes written on paper or spells can be folded and placed inside. In addition, a gemstone can be set into the wand's end, affixed with strong glue. Bamboo may be sanded down and painted or dyed in the user's choice of colors, or simply left green, yellow, or brown.

Hand-made wands are often a favorite choice among Wiccans, and making a new wand during a sabbath is a particularly well-loved practice.

The following is a chart of popular wood used in making wands, and the magical meanings of the wood:

- birch – feminine energy, healing emotional trauma, spells for renewal

- oak – sacred to the god, good for divination work, increases magical strength

- elder – intuition, linked to feminine energy, blessings, connection to the fairy realm

- ash – beloved to fairies; connected with justice and the dream realm

- alder – strengthens connections to the spirit realm, increases healing abilities; masculine energy, protection

- yew – connected to the cycles of death and rebirth, All Hallow's and Samhain, long life, psychic visions

- acacia – a protective wood, capable of enhancing psychic ability

- apple – good for money magic and abundance, love and romance

The Bell

Sound is one of the most powerful forces on Earth; it instantly instills in us emotion, be it powerful or peaceful. It is an instant call to prayer or focus. Bells are recognized and used throughout the world as a means to call the faithful home, or to redirect followers' attention from the mundane to the divine. A bell can be used to cleanse a space of negative energy, driving out unwanted vibrations so that a space can be filled with sweeter energetic attention. A bell can also be used to highlight or call attention to positive energy. As mortal beings, we are instantly effected by sound. Our brains shift in chemical balance, focus, and mood depending on the sounds we're listening to.

The bell is not considered one of the primary Wiccan tools, but it can be highly useful in ritual and in magic. You can ring a bell to call upon the God or the Goddess, use its tone to charge and/or cleanse other magical tools as well as crystals and candles, and you can use it to symbolize the beginning of magical work, or the end. Ringing a bell to induce ourselves into a more magically-conducive, meditative state is also a good practice.

An important thing to note is that the tools should match the user. When casting spells, look inward and note the different aspects of yourself. What calls your attention more: Earth or Fire, Air or Water? Whether you use the trailing smoke of a stick of incense, a hand-carved wooden wand, a shining athame, or the cool, calm tone of a struck bell to activate the magic in your spells is totally up to you.

With bells, it is perfectly acceptable to have a collection of them, as all bells sound somewhat different from each other. A bell is certainly something to purchase in person, so you can decide if the tone is pleasing to you or not.

The Besom

Another iconic symbol of the witch is, of course, the besom, otherwise known as the broom. The besom is used in Wicca to magically " sweep out" old, stagnant, and negative energy. The legend concerning witches and brooms and their ability to fly may have come from shamanic practices of astral projection. Otherwise, the besom is a fairly mundane tool with one specific purpose. Like the athame, it should not be used for general housekeeping, only magical cleansing. Hand-made besoms can be ordered online or found in craft, country, and magical supply shops. If you prefer to buy a regular broom and consecrate it as a besom, that's fine too.

The Boline

The boline is traditionally white-handled and single-bladed, and is kept sharp so it may cut herbs, handfasting ribbons, candles and wood. Some bolines are shaped like a crescent, while others are straight. The boline is still considered a sacred tool even if it's used for mundane activities. Just like the athame, there are many non-traditional varieties of the boline, and you can always consecrate your own.

The Book of Shadows, or Grimoire

A witch's book of shadows is where he or she records the magical work that has been cast, as well as spells they have written or newly-learned and their observances throughout. Any form of magical knowledge can be recorded here. It is important that the book never contain anything dark or harmful. Additionally, a grimoire should not be used to record anything mundane. It can be kept on the altar space regularly.

The Mortar and Pestle

A mortar and pestle is essential to those who wish to practice herbal magic. It can be helpful during spells that call for a variety of herbs to be mixed; as you grind the herbs together, chant words of magic, or picture the outcome of the spell that you desire to occur.

The Altar Cloth

Altar cloths can be purchased specifically from Wiccan and pagan shops, or hand-sewn; you can also use cloth, scarves, or tablecloths that appeal to you or are appropriate for the season and the sabbath.

Candles

This is an item that you will be in search of around the clock as a Wiccan. If you ever find that you do not have a particular color for a spell, know that a simple white candle can take the place of any other color. A good time to stock up on red and green candles is during Christmas and Valentine's Day; Halloween is a great time to stock up on black and orange candles. Websites such as Amazon also sell a wide variety of colored candles from sellers especially catering to pagans and Wiccan.

Chapter 6: A Beginner's Grimoire – Basic Spells to Master

The Responsibility That Comes With Magic

Some important concepts to learn before you begin practicing magic are as follows.

For Wiccans (as well as for many other pagans), magic is a gift, as well as a powerful tool. There is a great responsibility that coincides with becoming a witch and a Wiccan. There are people in the world who do not believe in magic, and who are not aware of the effects it can cause, the damage it can do, or the havoc in can wreak if not properly respected and utilized. Wiccans agree to never use their magic for ill or for harm. To do so would be a betrayal of their commitment to the natural world, to the divine, and to the God and Goddess. Not only that, but that ill-sent magic would return in triplicate, disrupting and devastating that Wiccan's life in ways no one can foresee.

With the gift and acceptance of magic comes the belief that all life is sacred. Even the person who cut in front of us on the highway, even the politician making the lives of the impoverished a misery, even our ex who stole half of our belongings. To be Wiccan is not to *lay down* and give up, however, and there are ways to handle the difficult aspects of life as well as troublesome people that do not directly harm them, nor bring harm back onto us triple-fold. With patience, reverence, respect, and the willingness to learn, we can avoid causing harm to ourselves and to others with our magical craft.

Take a seemingly innocent thing as a love spell. So many of us want true love in our lives, or even brief, exciting love—whatever's available, we'll take it! Wiccans are not always necessarily more " mature" then the next person, after all—we're human, right? Love is what makes life worth living, it is the joy and the beauty of the heart, of intimacy, and of human connection. It is the embodiment in the flesh of the divine Connection. That being said, there are so many love and attraction spells out there that get the concept of love magic simply *wrong*. And here's why.

When you seek to " bewitch" another into loving you, finding you attractive, or drawing close to you, you are breaking one of the most important rules of magic and witchcraft: you are bending another human being's *will*. Our will is sacred, and is a gift from the divine. It is what makes us unique and curious, powerful and courageous, and also capable of love. Without will, we are slaves to the energy of the universe, to the forces of the natural world, and to each other. How can love be born of enslavement? The answer is, it cannot. A spell, successfully cast, that turns another's heart towards you will only inevitably make that person unnaturally obsessed with the spellcaster, which is an uncomfortable situation for both parties. Obsession is not real love, and it wears the subject of the obsession down after a while. In time, both parties will grow to resent each other, and as the negative reaction to an unnatural connection builds, so will darker emotions such as hate and rage. Nobody wants to experience this in life, and in the end, the witch will be the one to suffer the most as the pain of this inauthentic bond and its inevitable destructions returns to them, triple-fold.

So, wait just a minute, you might ask—why *are* there so many love spells, then? The answer is simple: because everybody wants love, and very few of us want to wait for it. The world mistakenly views other people as objects; we live in a society where co-dependency is celebrated with t-shirts claiming " He's Mine" and other such philosophies of obsession and ownership. *True* love comes when it is ready, and it comes when it pleases to. If you want a tumultuous relationship of infatuation, that can often lead to lies, deception, and infidelity, then by all means, try your hand at a typical " love" spell. But I hope you reconsider.

Wicca provides us a with a loving framework of respect, consent, and self-awareness. We are not shamed for our desires—quite the contrary! Desire, attraction, and sex are simply a natural part of life, and nothing to be ashamed of, as long as we don't disrespect another person's personal boundaries in fulfilling our own needs, physical or emotional. What can we do when we desire another? There are many magical solutions to this problem. We can choose a night sacred to the Goddess and ask for guidance. We can cast a divination spell to see if perhaps this desired person is even right for us (or available). We can also divine to see if *we* are ready for love and intimacy—many times we believe we're ready, but actually still have a lot of work to do in the areas of personal development. It would be unfair to a new lover or partner to show up unprepared.

To be open to new, *true* love is an act of both honesty and courage. Casting a spell that examines one's self and one's heart, and takes time to understand everything that goes into a successful, happy union—whether it be long term or a brief dalliance—is a great work, and takes time to complete. When we consider reaching out to another person with love, we are taking a courageous first step. Making sure that our self-esteem and *empathy* are firmly in place is necessary and important, so that we don't get hurt in the process, and so that we do not hurt anyone else.

Magical aspects to focus on when considering spells of love, romance, and attraction are:

- What can I do to make myself feel more at ease around a potential lover?

- How can I make myself feel more attractive? What is blocking me? What are my strengths?

- How is my physical and emotional health? How can they be improved?

- What do I have to offer a potential partner? What would I need them to be able to offer to me?

Finally, all magic should be regarded with maturity and with humility. Magic is a beautiful, life-changing gift. Appreciate it, but always respect it.

Candle Magic

Candle magic is the most simple, yet often the most effective, type of magical spell anyone from a beginning witch to a ten-year master can cast. Candle magic combines the elements of Water and Fire to produce incredibly powerful results.

When preparing to perform a candle spell, first choose the color of the candle you need for the purpose of your magical work.

White candles are all-purpose, but can also be used in purification, blessings, cleansings, and spells to reveal the truth of a matter.

Black candles are used in divination, house cleansing, banishment, to rid a situation of a certain influence, and in binding.

Brown candles are used in Earth magic as well as fertility, grounding, balance, and to connect with nature and animal spirits.

Orange candles are used for abundance, success, attraction, raising energy, solar rituals, and to celebrate the harvest.

Red candles are used for love and attraction spells, virility, fire magic, and magic to boost self-confidence and strength.

Pink candles are used for love, beauty, and magic to bring peace to a volatile situation.

Purple candles are for Crone mysteries, divination, to connect with the scholarly God, and for spirit magic.

Green candles are used in money magic, to draw wealth, to attract benevolent nature spirits, and for good luck magic.

Blue candles are used in magic regarding the intellect such as good luck when taking a test, as well as Water magic.

1. Simple Candle Spell

You will need:

A candle

matches (sacred fire is best not lit with metal, such as a lighter, but if that's all you have then it will do)

a candleholder or dish

oil to consecrate the candle (Crown of Success or altar oil works well, but olive oil will do in a pinch) your athame or boline

Concentrate on your desire; choose a candle that coincides with what you want to achieve, such as green for money success, red for increased vitality and energy, pink for enhancing beauty, etc.

On a new, waxing, or full Moon, cast your circle and draw down the energy of the Moon. Feel it fill your circle with light. Using your athame or boline, carve two or more words describing your desire into the candle. Dab a few drops of consecrating oil on either side of the candle bring the oil towards you. Dab one drop of the oil on your forehead, near your third eye.

Light the candle.

Close your eyes and begin to visualize that which you desire coming true. When you are ready, open your eyes and watch the candle's flame. Say:

" Candle light, candle bright,

With magic bring my desire to life".

Say the Words of Casting, and when you are ready, open the circle and ground your energy, allowing the candle to burn down to completion. (If you must leave the candle unattended, move it to a metal sink, bathtub, or large steel pot where it can burn undisturbed. Always take extra care around animals and small children.)

2. Candle Spell For Luck

You will need:

An orange candle

matches

a candleholder or dish

cinnamon and clove oil (mix powdered cinnamon and cloves with almond or olive oil)

At midnight on a full moon, anoint the candle and light it, then say three times:

" Witch's laughter, sun and moon,

beneath the sky come to me soon,

good luck swiftly come to me,

by the deserts, by the sea."

Say the Words of Casting, and when you are ready, open the circle and ground your energy, allowing the candle to burn down to completion.

3. White Candle Blessing Spell

You will need:

An white candle

matches

a candleholder or dish

blessing oil or rose oil

On a new moon, cast a circle that encompasses your entire home (you can walk around the house or through each room if it's an apartment) anoint the candle and light it, then say walk through the house and say in each room:

" From dusk to dark, midnight to early light

dawn to noon, all goodness and peace will bless this room."

When you are finished, place the candle in the house's centermost room (or kitchen).

Say the Words of Casting, and when you are ready, open the circle and ground your energy, allowing the candle to burn down to completion.

4. Candle Spell For Employment

You will need:

A red and green candle

matches

two candleholders or dishes

Crown of Success, or frankincense oil

athame, boline, or pin

On a waxing moon and on a Thursday, and only after you've actually applied for the job, cast your circle and carve the name of the company you wish for a position with on one side of the green candle, then carve an arrow pointing up on the other side. On the red candle, carve your name on one side, and the upward-pointed arrow on the other side. Anoint both candles and light them.

Say:

" I will succeed in getting the job I applied for at (company), (state the date)."

Say the Words of Casting, and when you are ready, open the circle. Allow the candle to burn for thirty minutes, then snuff it out with a pencil, by pinching it with your fingers, or with a metal candle snuffer. Each Thursday, burn the candles again, this time for 15 minutes, until you get the job.

When you get the job, discard the candle and leave a dish of milk and honey outside for the spirits.

5. Candle Blessing Spell

You will need:

a white candle

matches

a candleholder or dish

blessing oil or rose oil

On a new moon, cast a circle that encompasses your entire home (you can walk around the house or through each room if it's an apartment) anoint the candle and light it, then say walk through the house and say in each room:

" From dusk to dark, midnight to early light

dawn to noon, all goodness and peace will bless this room."

When you are finished, place the candle in the house's centermost room (or kitchen).

Say the Words of Casting, open the circle and ground your energy, allowing the candle to burn down to completion.

6. Simple Candle Divination Spell

You will need:

a purple, black or brown candle (white will do if these are not available); make sure the candle is not " dripless".

matches and a candleholder

a penny and a nickel

a large plate

rose or sandalwood incense

On a dark, new, or full moon, cast your circle and place the candle in its holder on the large plate. Place the nickel on one side and the penny on the opposite side of the candle. Designate which coin will mean " yes" and which coin will mean " no". (Write it down in case you forget the next day). Light the incense. Ask the question you want the answer to, then say four times:

" Candle burning bright, bring the truth to light."
As you say this each time, make a figure eight with
the lit incense over the entire plate. When you are
done, snuff out the incense, say the Words of
Casting, and when you are ready, open the circle
and ground your energy, allowing the candle to
burn down to completion. The next day observe
the candle, and whether the spell answered your
question with a " yes" or a " no".

7. Walnut Spell For Money

You will need:

a walnut

a dollar bill

cinnamon oil

Crown of Success oil

green yarn

a pair of scissors or your boline

a green candle that drips

matches

On a full moon, cast your circle and draw the power of the Full moon. Anoint the walnut with the oil, then carefully wrap the dollar bill around it. Secure the entire bundle with the green yarn, wrapping it seven times and tying it in three knots. Light the candle and allow it to drip a few times onto the walnut/money bundle. Snuff out the candle and put aside, then hold the walnut charm and say:

" Money, money come to me,

by the power of three times three,

from Sun, the Moon, the forest and sea

with harm to none and effortlessly"

Say the Words of Casting, open the circle and ground, then place the lucky walnut outside or in a windowsill to finish charging under the full moon's light. Whenever you are home, place this charm on or near your wallet to draw money to it the next day.

8. Juniper Berries Spell

You will need:

7 juniper berries

a circle of green cloth

green yarn

On a Sunday on either the new or waxing moon, gather the berries into the cloth and tie them tightly. Carry the berries in your pocket for 7 days; on the seventh day, toss the berries onto a cross section of two streets. You will have good luck for the rest of the month.

9. Mojo Bag

You will need:

Orange, purple, or green cloth and yarn or a small cloth bag in any of those colors

basil

oregano

thyme

rosemary

a lodestone

a golden dollar

white quartz

blessing, rose, or Crown of Success oil

a white candle

matches

a dish or candleholder

On a full moon, gather the ingredients together in the bag or on the cloth after you've cast your circle. Add a few drops of the oil, then secure tightly. Light the candle after anointing it with the oil, and say:

" Lucky mojo bless this charm

to bring success and cause no harm

give me luck in love and money

as good as gold and sweet as honey."

Say the casting words, open the circle, and ground your energy. You can either carry the bag with you or leave on your altar. Allow the bag to further charge beneath the light of the full moon.

10. Spell to Open Your Heart to Love

You will need:

a pink candle

matches

a candleholder or small plate

three red or deep pink roses

pink quartz or amethyst

a clear glass bowl or cauldron filled with water

On a new, waxing, or full moon, cast your circle and light the pink candle. Set the crystal in the water, then take one of the roses. Pluck the petals off, one by one, and add them to the water. Each time you pluck a petal say one of these affirmations until you are done:

" I am ready for true love to come into my life.

I am willing to work to be a good partner and friend.

I am not afraid of love.

I am not afraid of being loved, nor am I afraid of giving love.

Each moment spent with my love will be treasured; I will not pine their absence but look forward to their return.

Love requires stability. I will look to the Earth for guidance.

Love requires emotion. I will look to the Water for healing.

Love requires communication. I will look to the Air for clarity.

Love requires passion. I will look to the Fire for inspiration."

Repeat these affirmations until all petals are in the water. Raise up the bowl and state calmly and happily, " I am ready for love. When love is ready, that it should it come to me willingly, so mote it be." Say the Words of Casting and leave the bowl on the altar overnight. The following morning, remove the crystal and discard the contents in the yard or street.

11. Protection Jar (Witch's Jar)

You will need:

a mason jar

white vinegar

rusted nails and pins

small pieces of broken glass and mirror

a piece of your hair and nail clippings

a black candle

matches

clove oil

This spell diverts negative energy that was intended for you, to be trapped forever in this bottle. You can bury the bottles in your yard, or hide them in a pot covered in soil. They should be placed outside your home if you can, but near the door or under the kitchen sink works also.

On a waning moon, cast your circle then fill the bottle with all of the ingredients. Anoint the candle with clove oil. Cloves can be used in luck and money magic, but they also greatly reduce gossip and slander. Melt the bottom of the candle a bit to adhere it to the lid of the mason jar.

Say:

" By the stirring of the moon, throughout the Year, from June to June,

by dark of night and light of day,

whatever enemies may send or say,

becomes like dust, and floats away,

to never return, nor hurt, nor burn.

Within this bottle ever trapped,

ill will dispelled, and fury sapped,

ended, erased, tricked, and trapped."

Speak the Words of Casting, open the circle, ground, and place the bottle where you're able to, then give it no more of your thought.

12. Healing Bath

You will need:

a pale blue, lavender, white, or pink candle

matches

a candleholder or small dish

rose or chamomile oil

white quartz

dried lavender

dried basil

dried chamomile

a tea infuser or cloth bag

Perform this ritual at any time other than the dark moon.

Because you are performing this ritual in your bathroom, you will need to cast your circle there. Anoint the candle with the oil while you draw a bath. Light the candle and place it where you can safely observe it. Add the herbs to the infuser or cloth bag, and drop these into the bathwater. Drop the quartz into the bath as well, then add three drops of the oil to the water.

Get into the bath, and gaze at the candle. Imagine the stress, pain, discomfort, and any sadness or stiffness begin to leave your body. Breathe deeply the healing power of the herbs and oil. As the candle flickers imagine the healing fire soothe your blood, erasing any malady or injury from your cells. Feel the ebb and flow of the ocean's tides in the water. You are one with the Earth, healed by the divine light. Remain as long as you like in the water, but stay for at least 15 minutes.

When you are finished, pat yourself dry from feet to head, discard the herbs and candle, and place the crystal on your altar.

Chapter 7: A Glossary of Magical Correspondences

This chapter is meant to help you in creating your own spells and rituals.

Plants, Herbs, and Flowers

A.

Acacia. Use in protection spells and to enhance psychic abilities. This is also known as Gum Arabic.

African violet. Protection magic, promotes joy in the home, used as incense on Ostara.

Agrimony. Helps the user get past mental blocks. Reduces or eliminates fear. Places a barrier against negativity and evil.

Alfalfa. A kitchen with a jar of alfalfa will never know poverty. Add alfalfa to money and prosperity spells to add a boost in power.

Allspice. An all around excellent herb for success, good luck, money, wealth. Also use in healing baths.

Almond. Prosperity, draws healing power from the God and the Goddess. Placed on the altar at Imbolc and Beltane.

Alyssum. Balances emotions and reduces anger.

Angelica. Divine energy. Purification, blessing and protection from harm. Put in shoes to give extra energy to your steps.

Apple. Sacred to the Goddess; when cut in half horizontally reveals a five-pointed star. Use in fertility magic and on Samhain.

Ash. Use for the Yule log. Ash leaves in water overnight prevents illness. Use in water magic, protection spells and luck spells.

Aster. Use for love and beauty magic, and for divination regarding true love.

B.

Balsam. Use in magic for increasing personal strength, in dream pillow sachets, and for incense.

Bamboo. Protects the user from hexes. Use in wish-making magic, for wands, and for good luck.

Basil. Anything from love to money magic, to restore clear thoughts, to protect from danger and in job searches. Protects a house from harm.

Bay Leaf. Use to make wishes, in purification spells, and when carried to protect against hatred and violence.

Bayberry. Used in candles to increase their potency. Also for good luck magic.

Benzoin. An incense resin used to purify, defeat ailments of the mind and spirit, and to consecrate an area.

Birch. Use in protection magic and to purify an area. If you plant a birch tree near your house it will protect the home from damage by lightning.

Blackberry. This plant is sacred to the goddess Brigid. Use for protection spells, money magic, and healing rituals and baths.

Blessed Thistle. Use to ward off negativity. Thistle kept in the home rejuvenates the interior energy.

Bloodroot. Found in the Appalachian mountains and used by Native Americans as an ink and dye, bloodroot can be used in love and purification magic. May be used as a symbol of blood in rituals, so as to not use the real thing. Sends hexes back to their sender.

Bluebell. Use in luck magic and to cultivate friendship.

Borage. Use to enhance courage and to encourage hope.

Buckeye. Carry one in your pocket for good luck in all endeavors and affairs. Use in divination magic and wealth charms.

Burdock. Used in ritual cleansing and for protection magic.

C.

Calendula. Use this flower for help in legal matters. Harvest at noon to use in spells to strengthen the spirit.

Cardamon. Use in magic regarding fidelity and love. Inspires desire.

Carnation. Use for protection and healing spells. Burn dry blossoms to encourage creativity.

Chamomile. Dream and sleep magic, sachets for healing and stress-reduction. Can be incorporated into money and love spells.

Cilantro. Keeps a garden safe from disease or misfortune. Makes a home peaceful.

Cinnamon. Money, love, and luck magic. Used in charms to draw wealth and success.

Clove. Use to reduce harmful gossip. Incorporate into money and love spells.

Clover, Red. Use clover water to consecrate tools. Also used in money and success magic, as well as love spells.

Coriander. Used in handfasting rituals and health magic.

Cowslip. Love and discovery of hidden, rich things. Enhances attraction and personal beauty.

D.

Daffodil. For use in fertility magic as well as good fortune and love spells.

Daisy. Magic for babies and children. Restores hope and innocence. Protection of children.

Dandelion. Used to connect with benevolent spirits, in purification, and in wish-making charms.

Dragon's Blood. This resin when burned is used to purify and amplify spellwork.

E.

Echinacea. Use in healing spells and increasing a spell's potency. Used in money magic and as an altar offering.

Elder. Good for magic promoting restful sleep and good dreams. Protection spells and warding against negativity.

Evening Primrose. Enhances beauty when used in a bath. Connects user with the fairie realm.

F.

Fern. Use for cleansing rituals, to purify altar tools, and for mental focus and clarity.

Feverfew. Healing rituals and protection against bad luck. Good for travelers.

Foxglove (poisonous). For magic regarding the Underworld, protection spells and divination magic.

Frankincense. Blessing a space or tools, for success in all endeavors, and for offerings at sabbaths.

G.

Gardenia. Use in spells to promote peace and keep negativity at bay. Brings comfort to those who are sick.

Garlic. Potent protection when used in sachets to guard the house. Sacred to Hecate. Used to capture illness and remove from the body.

Geranium. Banishes negativity and brings happiness to the home.

Ginger. For sexual energy, money and luck spells, and to use in mojo bags.

Goldenrod. Plant to attract money. When it blooms naturally by the front door, wealth is coming. Carry in pocket for 24 hours to reveal a secret crush.

H.

Hawthorn. Use to bring happiness to the heart. Use in floor washes to spiritually cleanse a home.

Heather. Used to make besoms. Use in protection and luck spells.

Hibiscus. For use in love and romance spells. Protects against ailments.

High John Root. Also called John the Conqueror. Used for money luck, personal strength, business success, and good luck while gambling.

Honeysuckle. Use in money sachets and to attract fast abundance. Promotes confidence and intuition. Enhances psychic ability.

Hyacinth. Use in spells for peace and restful sleep.

I.

Iris. Use in magic spells for wisdom as well as to bolster courage. Can be used to consecrate magical tools.

Irish Moss. Use to attract money and hold on to it. Increases the potency of a spell it's added to.

Ivy. For protection magic as well as fertility and healing. Use in love spells.

J.

Jasmine. Excellent when used in potions to cleanse and re-charge magical crystals. Flowers attract wealth and enhance beauty.

Job's Tears. These seed pods help with money magic, spells to find a new job, and are good when used in mojo bags.

Juniper. Use in luck and prosperity magic; attracts abundance and harmony.

L.

Laurel. Use in love spells and for protection; also used in weddings to bless the bride.

Lavender. Good for money, luck, prosperity, and love spells. An excellent healing herb. Lifts depression.

Lemon. Use to ritually cleanse a space and promote personal success.

Lemon Balm. Enhances spiritual growth. Used in love spells and to enhance the chances for success.

Lilac. Protects a home from wandering ghosts and harmful spirits. Use in spells regarding wisdom and good luck.

Lily of the Valley. Helps reconcile estranged couples. Use in spells for peace and happiness.

Linden Flowers. Mix with lavender in dream pillows to help fall asleep. Promotes positive spirituality.

Lovage. Use in banishing rituals and to attract love and desire.

M.

Magnolia. Use in love and beauty magic. Also helps with healing spells to overcome addictions.

Maple. Good for money and wealth magic and to promote longevity and good fortune.

Marigold. Solar rituals, money luck, and success in legal affairs.

Marjoram. Use to purify and ritually cleanse a space. Carry for money luck. Used in love spells and to protect the home.

Meadowsweet. Aids in job searches. Calms scattered nerves.

Mint. Raises energy and aids in communication. Helps a business attract new customers. Use in wealth and prosperity spells.

Mistletoe. For magical spells involving fertility, virility, creativity, and to promote good health.

Mugwort. For help with divinatory dreams and good rest. Use in healing magic and to promote psychic abilities.

Myrrh. To ritually cleanse and bless a space. Also used for money magic.

N.

Nettle. Wards evil and keeps negativity at bay. Use in tinctures to reduce gossip and pettiness.

Nutmeg. Use in prosperity and money spells. Carry in pocket to attract good luck.

O.

Oak. Sacred to the God. Good for wands and to promote harmony and good fortune in the home.

Orange. Use in spells for abundance and happiness in romantic relationships. Use in baths for beauty.

Oregano. Increases personal strength. Promotes joy. Adds energy to spells for luck and money.

P.

Palo Santo. Use to spiritually cleanse a space.

Parsley. Use for home protection. Promotes a balanced sense of self.

Patchouli. Use in money magic, for love spells, and stay grounded.

Periwinkle (poisonous). Promotes harmony in marriage. Use for money spells and obtain a sense of grace.

Pomegranate. Use for Samhain and Yule altars and in divination magic. Use to grant wishes. Also good for fertility and prosperity magic.

R.

Rose. Use for divine blessings in magic, to promote love and friendship.

Rosemary. Banishes evil and negativity. Purifies a space. Promotes clear thinking and success.

Rue. Enhances the potency of magical candles and potions.

S.

Saffron. Used as an aphrodisiac. For use in love magic and increasing happiness.

Sage. Use to spiritually cleanse a space. Write a wish on a leaf of sage and place it under your pillow. After three nights, if you recall dreaming about your wish, you can rest assured it will come true.

Sandalwood. Good for wands, healing magic, and to banish negativity.

Solomon's Seal. Used to cleanse a space and for spells with protection.

Star Anise. Use in money magic. Increases psychic ability.

T.

Tarragon. Use for healing after emotional distress.

Thyme. Good for money spellwork, increasing good luck, and to enhance one's good reputation.

V.

Valerian. Promotes restful sleep. Good for protection and spiritual cleansing in baths. Also good for love spells.

Vanilla. Good for love and attraction magic. Increases mental sharpness and memory.

Vervain. Used for protection magic and wealth spells.

Violet. Helps with headaches and restless sleep. Use in sachets for peace and restoring calm.

W.

Willow. Sacred to the Moon. Used for making wishes.

Wisteria. Use for prosperity spells and psychic abilities.

Woodruff. Good for luck and money. Use in protection spells.

Y.

Yarrow. An excellent healing spell. Increases courage.

Yerba Mate. Use in spells for fidelity and romantic love.

Crystals

Agate. protection magic, courage, enhances creativity and staying grounded.

Amber. Improves balance and increases positive energy. Connects with the ancestors.

Amethyst. Love and money magic. Raises spiritual connection.

Aquamarine. Water magic. Reduces fear and promotes restful sleep.

Beryl. Increases psychic ability. Good for strengthening relationships.

Bloodstone. Protects against calamity. Use for money magic and success in business.

Celestite. Divine energy and connection.

Citrine. Use in spells for abundance and prosperity.

Clear Quartz. Cleansing, clear thoughts, and blessings.

Emerald. Use to promote harmony between partners.

Garnet. Money and love spells, raises energy and vitality.

Hematite. Gathers negativity so that it's kept from entering you. Will break when full.

Jade. Money luck, instilling confidence, good for fertility spells.

Lapis Lazuli. Connection to ancestors. Increases creativity.

Lodestone. Good for mojo bags and money magic.

Malachite. Helps clears mental blocks.

Moonstone. Lunar magic.

Obsidian. Protection magic.

Onyx. Samhain altar, wealth spells.

Opal. Blessings and prosperity spells.

Peridot. Water magic. Invites positive change.

Petrified Wood. Connected to the Earth element.

Rose Quartz. Increases positive vibrations.

Numbers

1. The number **One** vibrates with the life-force of the universe. It stands for the first, for beginnings, and is represented by the Magician card of the Tarot. One can be looked at as a source of life, creation, and power. The Wiccan uses the number One to embark on journeys, and in spellcraft involved in beginnings, new relationships, courage, hope, and innocence.

2. **Two** is sacred to the union of the God and the Goddess. It represents both duality as well as polarity—twins as well as opposites. It is the solstices as well as the equinoxes, and is represented by the Lovers card of the Tarot. Use this number in love magic, for balance and understanding, and for magical endeavors regarding communication.

3. **Three** is regarded as the most sacred number of all. It is representative of the Triple Goddess as well as the three phases of life: birth, life, and death. It can also be thought to frame the essence of the planet Earth: air, water, and soil. Three is a highly flexible number and be used in spellwork for money and luck, for fertility, for action, as well as for neutrality and to regain calm.

4. **Four**, to Wiccans, is considered a number of foundation. It represents the four elements, the four directions, as well the four corners of a building. It is used in magic to begin something important as well as to spark creativity and to promote excellent, long-lasting work and relationships.

5. **Five** is the number of the pentagram and of humanity. It can also be seen as the elements if the element of Spirit is included. Five is highly magical, and when featured in the Tarot, can be symbolic of

energy itself and how unpredictable it can be, and often chaotic.

6. **Six** is the number of communication, choice, and connection. It is a solar number and is sacred to the Sun God. Also a masculine number, it brings power to the user in seeking what is desired.

7. **Seven** is considered the luckiest number, and is sacred to the Goddess. It is connected to the Moon, and is used in magical workings regarding divination, feminine mysteries, intuition as well as wisdom.

8. **Eight** is the number of infinity and balance. It is also the number of Saturn and of protection, though some connect it with Mercury and with communication.

9. **Nine** is the number of the heavens and the afterlife, and is the sum of the equation " three times three". It is extremely powerful and connects us to the divine. It can be used in magical work for completion and mastery.

Conclusion

Thank for making it through to the end of *Wicca For Beginners*, let's hope it was informative and able to provide you with all of the tools you need to achieve your goals whatever they may be.

The next step is to think about what you've discovered in this book and decide how you want to move forward in your exploration of Wicca. A good rule of practice is to get out into the natural world with an open mind. Take a day where there is no pressure or rush to get back to work or responsibilities. Observe the natural balance and energies around you, and see what catches your attention the most. There are messages hidden throughout the magical world that call to us through our subconscious mind; these will usually tell us what next to do on our spiritual journey.

On the next full moon, be bold and try your hand at casting a circle. You do not have to perform any magic; just light a simple candle and watch the flame dance as you sit with your thoughts in quiet contemplation. Feel the energy of the full Moon bless your sacred circle with divine, healing light. Record your thoughts and feelings, perhaps in a new grimoire. Write down goals and aspirations, and things you are curious to try within the framework of the Craft.

Finally, if you found this book useful in any way, a review on Amazon is always appreciated!

Printed in Great Britain
by Amazon